TWICE OUT OF SIGHT

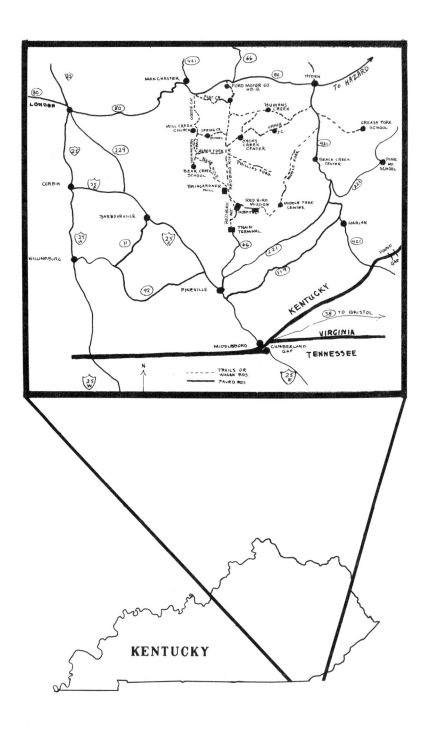

TWICE

OUT

OF SIGHT

REV. ROSCOE E. PLOWMAN

KENTUCKE IMPRINTS • BEREA, KENTUCKY   40403

DEDICATION

To Jessie, my wife, for her love, companionship and support through all of these years. Also Phyllis, Kent and Kay, our children who shared in many of these experiences.

ACKNOWLEDGEMENTS

I am indebted to Prosecuting Attorney James Pike, who after hearing some of my stories, urged me to put them in writing; to Raymond Nelson, M.D. and his wife Naomi for collaboration on stories in which they were involved; to Lawrence and Dorothy Chapman and Diana Bell for editing and typing the manuscript; to Lila Richards for her illustrations; to Everett Schaeffer, M.D. and his wife Roberta for their help in selecting and editing some of the stories; to Ruth Roark who listened to and concurred in this selection; and to Byron Crawford, *Courier Journal* columnist, for using some of the material in his column of February 5, 1982.

FOREWORD

Many interesting stories have been written about the people of southern Appalachia. Not all have come from a deep love and appreciation of the people.

Rev. Roscoe Plowman shares some vivid recollections of the people whom he served so effectively for twelve years. There is great pathos and heartache in some of his stories. But he also shares the joys and victories experienced by a man of God who has given much of his life in serving the people of the mountains. The unique humor of our people comes through in a beautiful way as they welcome a stranger from another part of the country and as they relate to one another.

"Preacher Plowman", as he is affectionately known by the many people whom he served in Leslie and Clay Counties, had a great influence on the lives of people of all ages. The stories he shares give us a good insight into the strong character and rich tradition of mountain people. There is much we can learn from them. The book will help preserve some elements of mountain culture which future generations will appreciate.

We commend this book to you knowing you will enjoy reading about the experiences of Roscoe and Jessie Plowman as they served the Lord in southeastern Kentucky.

E. T. Ehresman
Executive Director
Red Bird Mission, Inc.
Beverly, Kentucky

AUTHOR'S PREFACE

My maternal grandfather, a British subject born on Jersey Island, came to America in pre-Civil War days. Somewhere in the hills of Appalachia, he met and married Mary Morgan, a daughter of William Morgan who was a brother of "Raider" John Hunt Morgan. Grandpa became a citizen of the United States and being an admirer of that great Kentucky mountain statesman, Abraham Lincoln, voted for him when he ran for president. About the time the Civil War broke out, Grandma Mary's father joined his brother to ride with the "Raiders". Grandpa picked up his family and moved to Missouri to lessen the conflict between himself and his father-in-law. Mother was born here. He soon moved on to Western Oregon where he homesteaded in a remote valley near the ocean. I was born in the Oregon mountains and grew up in this pioneer environment.

When Jessie and I applied through our church for mission work, the bishop said, "Who else would fit into the environment of the Kentucky hills better than Roscoe who is himself a mountaineer?" Thus we were appointed to serve at the Jacks Creek Center of Red Bird Mission in December 1936. Even though speech, customs and ways were somewhat different, we soon were made to feel that this was home.

I have wanted to share with others part of our experiences for some time; especially the genuine acceptance of us, the love, hospitality (cleverness), wit, humor, pioneer spirit, pride, resourcefulness, faith in God and the ability to accept good fortune or tragedy as it came to them. We did as Paul admonished in Romans 12:15, "Rejoice with those that do rejoice, and weep with those that weep."

After delving into my memories I have written down some of our experiences and some of the stories, many humorous, that they have shared with me at their hearth side.

I wanted to be sure that I would not offend or embarrass anyone and have used ficticious names in some cases. I drove back to the area where we spent those twelve wonderful years. I was overwhelmed by the smiles, hugs and warm handshakes that greeted me, and the many invitations to "Take the night." One man introduced himself and said: "I'm Daugh Sizemore. I was one of the boys that threw the skunk under the school-house when your daughter, Phyllis, was teaching. She made us crawl under and pull the skunk out. She was strict but a good teacher and I liked her."

Edith Asher is the postmaster now, having taken over when her mother, Ruth Roark, retired. As I visited with her, a man came for mail that said, "I remember you. You rode up Bear Creek and bought a young sheep from me. You gave me three dollars and I wondered how you would get a live sheep home. You just tied its feet together, laid it across the horse behind the saddle and rode off."

Doctor Everett and Roberta Schaeffer shared some of their busy time to screen and edit the manuscript so that it would be acceptable to the area. I got the clearance I needed from Supt. Ed Eheresman and subjected the material to one more test. If Ruth Roark accepted it, I knew I could go ahead and publish. We talked about it and old times for two hours. She not only approved, but gave me a picture to put in the book of herself and her youngest son, Raymond, standing in front of the old post office. Ruth said, "You know, I had hoped you and Jessie would build here when you retired." All of Ruth and Leonard's children, like most mountain youth when given a chance, have done well. Herman graduated from college cum laude, went on to get a master's degree and with his wife also teaching, became one of the principals in Dayton, Ohio. The others are car-

X

penters, electricians, contractors and postmaster. Hundreds of our youth have gone out to be successful in many of the high professions. Some have returned to Red Bird as teachers, school superintendents, nurses, technicians and to fill other staff positions.

An old saying on Jacks Creek was, "Once you get your feet wet in the waters of Jacks Creek and leave, you will come back." Many have. I felt the tug in my own heart and poet, James Still expressed this feeling in his poem *White Highways*.

I have gone out to the roads that go up and down
In smooth white lines stoneless and hard.
I have seen distances shortened between two points,
The hills pushed back and bridges thrust across
The shallow river's span.
To the broadways, and back again I have come
To the creek-bed roads and narrow winding trails
Worn into ruts by hoofs and steady feet,
The far between, the slow arrival.
Here is my pleasure most where I have lived
And called my home.[1]

Roscoe Plowman

---

[1]James Still, *Hounds On The Mountain* (New York 1937) p. 45.

CONTENTS

PART 1
THE FIRST TIME AROUND

PART II
SECOND TIME AROUND

PART I

THE FIRST TIME AROUND

CHAPTER I

ANIMALS THAT GRUNT AND SQUEAL IN THE NIGHT

The years before the Kentucky legislature made it illegal for stock to run loose in the hills, herds of hogs roamed the creeks and hollers. Some were much like the old razorbacks and wild in nature. Gradually, these were being replaced by better breeds. Red Bird Mission was involved in raising pedigreed hogs and distributing the weaned pigs to many families.

Hogs survived in the hills by living on roots and grubs. When fall came, they fattened up on the acorns and beech mast. A hog chosen for butchering was penned up and fed slop and corn for several weeks to whiten and firm up the lard. Lard was an essential to mountain cooking.

You may wonder how each family knew its own hogs that ranged freely with others. Much like cattle that were branded on open range, each family knew its hogs by a system of markings. Each owner would take a sharp knife and notch, slit, or crop the ears of the unweaned pigs. Each owner then would see by the cuts on the right or left ears which hog was his. It was a criminal offense to take a hog with someone else's brand. Juries often considered the stealing of another man's livelihood as serious as taking another man's life.

I learned the brands of the owners of the hogs that roamed past the Jacks Creek Center. It made me think of our people who were still carrying the brand of Satan and how that when we are redeemed (bought) by the blood of Christ, the brand is changed to His markings. As the apostle Paul stated in Galations

6:17, "I bear in my body the marks of the Lord Jesus."

Visitors who came and stayed all night often asked in the morning, "What was that strange sound like rocks hitting together we heard last night?" We explained that when the creek was low in summer and the nights cool, the hogs would go up and down flipping the flat stones over with their snouts to hopefully find a juicy crawdad. Thus the steady "plop, plop, plop" of the rocks at night.

The most annoying noises of the hogs were on cold winter nights. There was an overhanging cliff across from our house where the hogs gathered for shelter. Since there were too many hogs to all get under the rock ledge, the ones out in the cold would climb over the others to find a warmer place, squeezing others out into the cold. A great deal of grunting and squealing went on all night as they pushed and rooted each other.

The racket disturbed our guests. We soon got used to it and slept soundly. Life on Jacks Creek was never dull.

CHAPTER II

CALLED TO KENTUCKY

Jessie and I had just completed four years in our first pastorate in Western Washington when the appointment came to serve as missionaries in the hills of Eastern Kentucky. I had grown up in an isolated community on the west coast of Oregon of pioneer parents and grandparents. My bishop contended that we had the ideal background to fit into the isolated life of Appalachia.

The day after Christmas in 1936, we loaded our few belongings and with Phyllis—our three year old daughter, boarded the Union Pacific at Portland for Chicago. Here we took another train south to Corbin, Kentucky, where once again we transferred. This time we boarded an antique L & N passenger-freight combination. Each passenger coach had the luxury of a pot belly coal stove for warmth; yet the passengers kept most of the windows open. The tobacco-stained stoves poured soot and smoke into the following cars along with the belching smoke from the coal burning locomotive. The train was filled with miners and mountain folks either walking the aisles or sitting on the blackened seats that at one time had been a beautiful red velour.

Those around us could see that we were "Furriners" and watched us with curiosity, especially the "Younguns". I was engrossed with watching the hills closing in around us as we switched into small mining towns to discharge and pick up passengers and freight. I listened to the strange accent and vocabulary of those around us and wondered: "How can we ever learn the ways of our new people and be accepted by them?" Amidst hissing steam and grinding brakes, we eventually rolled into Pineville, the small county seat of Bell County, nestled between high craggy ridges. This was Daniel Boone country near where he crossed Cumberland Gap into Kentucky.

Our new superintendent, a large jolly man, was there to meet us and welcome us to Kentucky. He pointed out the main tourist attraction, "Chained Rock," a huge rock perhaps a hundred feet high that had at one time split away from the main mountain, and looked as though it might topple across the highway far below. A giant chain (each link weighing many pounds) had been anchored to the top of the rock and stretched across to the cliff to give the appearance of the rock being held from falling.

Superintendent Lehman had some business, and we were free to look through the shops and stores. This was an enjoyable

Dr. Lehman, Supt. of the Red Bird Mission
in the early thirties and forties.

experience for me as each sales girl would ask, "What fur ye, honey?" Jessie had some difficulty getting me out of the stores to find a place to eat lunch. As we sat down at a table, a not-too-neat-looking waitress came up to us with pad in one hand and pencil in the other, swiping her pencil hand across her runny nose and down her apron, queried, "What fur ye, honey?" We settled for coffee and little else except milk for Phyllis. You didn't learn to drink mountain coffee in a day. If you had curly hair, it would take the kinks out. Mountain folks didn't waste their coffee grounds. The pot sat on the stove and as more coffee was needed, more grounds and water were added. When the pot was nearly half full of grounds, it was emptied and a fresh start was made. I finally got used to it and liked it.

The old Continental Hotel was a luxury in those days, so we settled down hopefully to rest up for a hard trip the next day. Being New Year's Eve, there was considerable celebration with firecrackers and guns going off all night long. The stories of shootings and feudin' we had heard didn't ease our minds any, and I was glad when morning came.

After a good breakfast in the hotel dining room, we were ready for the train trip up Straight Creek. Superintendent Lehman filled us in on some of the mountain customs as we rode along. At the end of the line we transferred to the waiting Bringardner Lumber Company train for the trip over the mountain.

We arrived at Beverly on the Bringardner Lumber train.

This time we sat on our luggage on an open flat car. The little lumber train puffed and tugged up one incline to the first switchback and then pushed to the next, sometimes crossing high trestles. Finally, we descended to Red Bird Valley below and our mission headquarters. What flat land we could see was filled with schools, dormatories, staff homes, office and hospital. Staff members were at the superintendent's home to greet us. A warm meal, true Kentucky hospitality, and genuine Christian fellowship made us glad we had come. What an introduction to Kentucky, but it was far from over.

Beverly Headquarters

CHAPTER III

A MANSION IN THE WILDERNESS

The evening festivities over, we were shown to our room on the second floor. Phyllis was already sound asleep, and as we turned out the light, the patter of rain on the roof turned to a downpour. The roar lasted most of the night and by morning had ceased. But there was a new sound as we arose. In the early morning light we could see and hear water rushing down the hillsides into the streams that were overflowing onto the schoolyard and playgrounds and dashing on down to form a roily churning river as it rushed past the hospital. A flood? No, a "Tide" in mountain terminology. We were anxious to get to our Jack's Creek center ten miles down river. No chance today. Maybe tomorrow. Headwater streams run off fast, so, sure enough, by the next day we were on our way. The early lumber train took us three miles to the large Bringardner steam sawmill. A commissary, boarding house and post office were here. The large payroll was a boon to this area during these deep depression days. Since our mountain people were strongly Bible oriented, the story was told that when the mill was ready to operate, it was decided to try out the big steam whistle. As the shrill blast echoed up and down the Redbird hollers and branches just before daylight, those who were not already up, sprang out of bed and one woman shouted: "Get up, Sam. The Lord has come and Gabriel is blowin' his trumpet!"

The leading Jack's Creek merchant and loyal church leader was waiting for us with his freight wagon and husky mule team.

Leonard and his wife, postmaster, Ruth, were to become our
staunchest friends.

Bringardner Lumber Mill—1940

Leonard's oldest boy, Herman, was with him to help us load.
There were many experiences ahead that this young man and I
would share together. After Jessie and Phyllis were safely
bundled in the buckboard seat of the wagon, Leonard climbed
aboard and with a resounding slap of the reins, the team leaned
into the harness and the wagon started its jolting seven mile
trip down the rocky road. As I watched I thought, "There go all
of my earthly possessions." Herman and I started walking,
jumping aboard the wagon to cross the deepest fords. Logs
were hauled out of Phillips Fork three miles from Jack's Creek
on makeshift tracks. At each river crossing instead of building
a trestle they ran the rails through the water. These crossings
had to be repaired after every "Tide". Our doctor had a small

rail car scooter that was a boon to Jack's Creek in times of emergency. It sometimes jumped the track but Doc would get off and set the car back on and proceed. Finally, the wagon turned up Jack's Creek away from the river. The road was notably smoother. Crews of men with picks and shovels and wheelbarrows were working on it as part of President Roosevelt's work program. The men leaned on their tools to curiously watch us go by, wondering what the new preacher was going to be like.

"Doc" making house calls—
Raymond Nelson on the gasoline rail car "Arabella"
1936-1940

The old parsonage had been struck by lightning and burned. A pretentious two story building with full basement had just been finished. It was the only home in the area with indoor plumbing, hardwood floors throughout; fully wired for electricity; a coal furnace, also a coal-burning cooking range and kerosene refrigerator. A gasoline generator charged the two rows of glass batteries to give us thirty-two-volt lights. Coils in the furnace heated our water. One room with a side door was designated as the clinic. We kept first aid supplies, medicines, and a large supply of drugs locked in a cabinet. We treated what we could. We called the doctor if the line was up to get advice for some cases. The doctor spent the day once a month and people came from everywhere to see him. They appreciated the medical help they received in this isolated valley. "Doc" even pulled teeth.

It was my job to keep the phone lines up. I kept climbers, wire, insulators, etc., ready to carry on my saddle when the line was out. Fallen trees, limbs and vandalism were the biggest problems. The wire made excellent clothes lines. It was difficult to convince some that the phone line was their "Lifeline" in emergencies. We were determined to show our people that the "Mansion" in cabin country was not to isolate us but to be their haven in time of need or just to come and visit.

I suppose one of the biggest barriers to folks feeling free to come in was that we had no open grate, pot bellied stove or bucket to spit into. I realized the problem better one day when Mary, our next-door neighbor, stopped at the gate to ask about Jessie, who had not been feeling well. I urged her to come in and visit but she declined by giving some excuse. "O, come on, Mary. It'll do her a lot of good for you to come in and sit a spell," I pleaded. At last she said, "Wal, all right," and turning her back she spit out a big chaw of her favorite twist and wiping her mouth with her apron, walked into the house. It took time but the "Mansion" barrier finally began to crumble.

Jacks Creek parsonage—The "Mansion" built in 1936.

CHAPTER IV

THE WAKE AND THE PREACHIN'

We were barely settled when the mother of one of our faithful members died. A casket had been carefully made from rough-sawed yellow poplar boards that were stored for just such an occasion. The store had bolts of black or grey cloth for the lining. Each casket was made to size. Narrow at the head, wider at the shoulders and tapering to the feet. Just two measurements were needed; length of body and width of the shoulders. No undertakers could get here, so no embalming was done. There was a wake and immediate burial. A graveside funeral would be held after crops were "Laid by" and a large meetin' could be announced with as many preachers as possible preaching. A rectangular box was made for the casket to fit into with a second lid for it. As soon as the box was being finished other men were already digging the grave. The hole was about a foot wider than the outside box and dug to about five feet in depth. Another hole the size of the box was dug at the bottom of the larger hole. The box was fitted into it leaving a ledge of dirt on either side for cross beams to be laid to carry the weight of the dirt. This was quite an art, and certain men of the community were depended upon to get the task done.

This was my first burial experience. It was taken for granted I knew about the Wake. I didn't.

I had been to the home just across the branch earlier and, thinking all was over until the following day, I came home. Just after dark, a strange rising, falling, wailing, and singing drifted across the air. "Here we have a time of weeping, pain and anguish on life's way. But in Heaven ther'ill be no sorrow. God shall wipe the tears away." I hastily donned a jacket and rushed back over to the home.

It was a well-built home—two rooms and a kitchen. A coal range warmed the kitchen. Beds, hickory bottom chairs, and a coal grate were in each of the rooms. The place was filled with people, sitting on chairs or floor and standing viewing the corpse in the casket by the open window. In the flickering light of kerosene lamps I could see wide-eyed younguns, babies nursing in mother's laps, men in overalls talking low and punctuating their sentences with the SST of tobacco juice hitting the live coals in the grate. Most of them I had not yet met. They nodded politely or shook my hand.

A mountain preacher had come and after singing "Will the Circle Be Unbroken", Preacher Boone got up to speak. I had never heard mountain style preachin' before. I had a lot to learn. Boone started slowly and deliberately, but as he gained momentum and "Got under the Power" as the people expressed it, words were tumbling from his lips so fast he was sucking in his breath between each sentence. It ended as suddenly as it started. He wiped his brow, thanked the people, and sat down. All eyes turned to me. What would the new preacher have to say? I was on the spot. To try to imitate Preacher Boone would be unthinkable, though I had been impressed with his sinsere presentation of the Word. So as sincerely and lovingly as I could, I quoted comforting Scriptures and shared my hope of Eternity. I had a feeling I had fallen far short of their expectations. Yes, I had much to learn.

The next day the casket was carried on the shoulders of strong men across Jack's Creek and up the hill to the grave plot. The casket was rested on the fresh pile of dirt beside the open grave. Several mountain songs were sung; I led in prayer. A man with a hammer pulled the four nails holding the lid down and the body was viewed again for the last time. There was much weeping and comforting of one another.

Finally, willing hands put the lid back in place and the young man began hammering eight penny nails through the lid into the casket sides eight inches apart completely around it. I cringed at each hammer blow feeling the hurt of the loved ones. But Mountain People are strong. They believe that what happens is God's will and with a "So be it" attitude, carry on.

Again designated men lowered the casket into the open box below, nailed down its cover and placed the split timbers across before shoveling the dirt back into the grave. This was the raw pioneer way to bury the dead; no soft music, flowers, green carpeting, silk-lined casket or bronze vault. They did the best they could with what they had, and that was sufficient.

Mountain burial of an infant.

CHAPTER V

EMERGENCY! EMERGENCY!

The feeding finished and the cow milked, I came into the house to hear Jessie calling urgently from the bedroom. She was hemorrhaging and the sheet was crimson. I almost panicked, but her calm instructions helped me to get my head together. I got more sheets and called for the teachers. Then I managed to get our mission doctor on the line. He said he would meet me at Phillips Fork.

Dr. Raymond Nelson
1936-40

Saddling Dixie and our neighbor's mule, I mounted and, with the mule tied to my saddle, dashed off for the doctor. Dixie sensed the urgency and galloped through the fords; the old mule, reluctant at first, finally decided it was better to run than to get his head jerked off. We made good time, but Doc was already there waiting for us. As we galloped our lathered mounts back towards Jack's Creek, I had visions of being too late and Jessie bleeding to death. The Devil kept nagging, "Where is your faith now?" Don't think I wasn't praying. I believed in putting action with my prayers. Doc was used to such emergencies and had a good hunch as to what was happening.

Jessie and I were not aware that she was pregnant. The hard jolting wagon ride from Brigardner to Jack's Creek was too much and the two-month-old fetus had been loosened enough that it finally aborted. I thanked God I still had my companion and my little daughter. We had struggled through some rough times together, including the worst depression, and we looked to share many more experiences; mostly good, some bad. We knew that "all things work together for good to them that love God, to them who are called according to His purpose." (Romans 8:28)

Jessie came through the ordeal with flying colors. She was weak, of course, but the Doctor left instructions on how to regain her strength, and we headed back to his rail car.

Raymond Nelson and his wife, Naomi, were about our age and our experiences together the next four years tied us in a bond of friendship that lasts to this day. Doc taught me a lot about administering medicine and patient care, and when he was in the Jack's Creek area, you might see us together gigging frogs along the river, riding Maude and Dixie on house calls, or trying out the old muzzle loading rifle a mountain pioneer had given me. I suppose I am most grateful for his saving my life.

I loved the way mountain women cooked. I had never en-

Dr. Raymond Nelson
Naomi and Bobby

joyed eating green beans, especially if they were dumped out of a can and warmed up. But take a mess of cornfield beans or half runners that have beans in them, cook them with a piece of hog jowel until they are soft and ummm they are good! If families didn't have hogs that ran wild around their home, they bought lard by the fifty pound stand. Lard was essential to mountain cooking. But my system finally rebelled.

Jessie had barely regained strength from her ordeal when we decided it was time to have "Open House". Living in the "Mansion" among the cottages and cabins posed a barrier to our being accepted as just common folk.

We set a Monday night for everyone to come and have a good time. Jessie and the teachers prepared "Goodies" and I planned some simple games. In planning the parsonage there should have been one coal grate included. Both men and women loved their "chawin' backy" but there was no place to spit. Some had never been in our home and were awed when they saw the varnished oak floors, the large picture windows with drapes, and the fancy wallpaper. This was a far cry from the more remote cabins, some even without floors and only the thin walls covered with old newspapers or catalog pages given them by the mission. Most of our community homes were well built, neatly papered and painted. I still question the good judgment of those who decided to build as large a structure as we had in such an isolated place.

Each weekend after coming home from staying in one of our mountain homes, I began having attacks of stomach cramps and abdominal pain. Jessie's greaseless cooking would ease the problem each time. But the Monday of Open House, tha pain did not go away and by evening the nausea had sent me to bed. People began arriving and were seated everywhere. The spacious stairwell made good balcony seats for the children. It sounded like everyone was having a good time. Jessie called up to me: "Do you think you could possibly come down for a while, Honey?" One of our concerned church members came up and with his help I dressed and joined the party somewhat pale and covered with a cold sweat. I helped with some games I had prepared. We gave out prizes and the folks got the message, I believe, that we truly liked them and wanted to be a part of their lives and for them to be a part of ours. It was a long evening for me. I finally got back to bed and slept some.

By morning the pain had settled to the lower right area of my abdomen. It was hard and too sore to touch. Jessie tried to ring the hospital for this was clinic day and Doc would be there. She turned the crank time and again, two longs and a short. Over and over again. The line was dead to ringing. But there was a hum, so one wire was still up. If someone would try to call from the hospital they could probably hear Jessie's voice. She sat by the phone most of the day with the receiver to her ear. Finally, one of the nurses started talking to another staff member in Beverly. Jessie yelled into the speaker and they heard her. The message was received. Doctor would be at Phillip's Fork about dark—would someone bring a mount? One of our young people saddled Dixie and, leading the old mule, was waiting for Doc when he arrived. Raymond said, "Roscoe, I believe you are having an acute attack of appendicitis. We need to get you to the hospital as fast as we can." He gave me a shot of morphine. What wonderful relief from the pain I had endured for two days.

Transporting a patient to the hospital in 1940.
I was carried this way when I had an appendictis attack in 1937.

If the appendix burst, the resulting peritonitus could be fatal. This was about a year before the Sulfa "Wonder Drugs" were introduced. The night was chilly and the river was up some from the recent rains. Yet, when the call went out, men gathered quickly. Some even came who were recovering from the flu. I must be carried on their shoulder three miles in and out of the river through the darkness. I was placed snugly wrapped on the litter and lifted to willing shoulders. Jessie walked alongside with the dozen or so men who were to take a turn spelling each other. Most had miners' caps fitted with flaring carbide lamps. It was a ghostly procession. As I lay on my back and watched the flickering shadows made by the passing branches of overhanging trees, and listened to the subdued voices of the men, I felt the quiet calmness, the serenity that comes when God is near. He was up there where I could see a few stars breaking through the clouds; yea, more than that, He was here among these brave men who were steadying me and each other as they plunged into the first cold river crossing. The water was swift and nearly thigh high. Jessie kept along with them as they supported her through the fords.

Three miles seems much longer on a rough winter night like that than it does when spring flowers are pushing through the leaves deposited by fall winds, and the sun is sparkling on the rippling stream and it is mating time among the birds. But at last, the final ford and I was carefully deposited on the little rail car.

The men wished me well. They had done what they could for their preacher. Jessie found a place where she could steady me if the car derailed as sometimes happened. Raymond started the

Red Bird Hospital at Beverly headquarters.

motor and we were on our way the seven miles left to the hospital. The only light now was a small flashlight to watch for limbs that might have fallen on the tracks. The end of the trip came at last, and willing staff hands carried me up the hospital steps to the "Prep" room. A quick white cell blood count confirmed Doc's diagnosis, and I was prepared for sugery while Doc scrubbed. The offending appendix was skillfully removed, badly swollen, but in time. It was now 2:00 A.M. My life had been spared and I had many to thank. God wasn't through with Jessie and me yet.

CHAPTER VI

CIRCUIT RIDING PREACHER

Over four hundred hours a year in the saddle and over twelve hundred miles a year of horseback trails over hills, ridges, hollers, streams and rivers was the schedule for the Jack's Creek Circuit when we arrived. I took a few meals standing up until I was toughened-in to riding once again. I acquired the outgoing preacher's mount, Dixie, a hard-riding three-year-old pacing mare. She could cover the ground faster when she was pacing, but it was a rough gait for the rider. Dixie was so full of life she would rear and prance when I took her from the stall, but when saddled and I was on board, she knew I was boss. A pair of leather saddle bags across the saddle carried my Bible and overnight gear.

Dixie and I

Dixie knew all the routes. If I headed her up Asher's Fork, she knew she would be spending the night in Hubbards' barn twelve miles away on Mill Creek. If I turned up Old House Branch, she would have a short, six mile trip to Napier's barn. Spring Creek meant eight miles to the head of the creek and Paw Lewis' barn. Down river was the longest run of fifteen miles. But to Dixie it was getting to stay in the spacious Ford Motor Company barn and to feast on grain and soybean hay instead of corn fodder and nubbins. Here Mr. Queen, the company administrator, was my host.

The Ford Motor Company owned much of Leslie County and parts of Clay and Bell Counties. The Company was in the business of acquiring timber and coal land by buying individual homesteads and leaving the former owners stay on for life for a small rental fee. Many who refused to sell were taken to court one by one and the Company, armed with old Virginia land grants, usually won.

A native had been hired by the Company to ride over the territory and see that the annual rental was paid and no living trees were cut. The tenants repaired their own cabins. The Company representative was a pleasant fellow who sometimes stopped with us to check on the forest-fire fighting equipment kept in our barn. It was commonly told that he was very generous with the widows and others who had difficulty paying their rent.

The trails sometimes became icy and slick in the winter. Regular nails were pulled from horse and mule shoes and replaced with sharp-headed ice nails for better traction. There was a rugged beauty of mountain trails even in winter. The leafless hardwood forests seemed to be clinging closer together for warmth. Water seeping from jutting cliffs formed glassy ice columns and cascades. Splashing in and out of the streams caused icicles to form on Dixie's fetlocks, making a tinkling sound as she jogged along. On such days, Jessie would meet me with a stick to knock the ice from my boots that had been frozen in the stirrups so I could dismount.

Spring, of course, was my favorite time to ride my circuits. The trees were getting new dresses of many shades of green. The tall poplars wore corsages of orange and yellow tulips. Delicate white lace of sarvis blossoms like petticoats were showing, while redbuds were blushing in the thickets. Dogwoods formed white displays and a myriad of sweet williams, spring flowers of many colors and white trilliams covered the ground with a patterned carpet. Here and there colonies of may apples pushed their delicate pale green parasols through the fallen autumn leaves and opened them carefully to shed the spring rains.

The morning sun filtering its rays through the forest into the deep canyon to warm fruitful earth and sparkling in the clear running stream was like a gorgeous theater backdrop made by God Himself for the greatest of all concerts—the well-orchestrated harmony of notes and melodies bursting from the throats of hundreds of various colored song birds. I hated to leave, but I must not be late. As I mounted and rode on, the concert momentarily ceased while I added my voice: "I trust God, I know He cares for me, on mountain top or o'er the rolling seas. Though billows roll, He keeps my soul. I know my Heavenly Father cares for me."

When I reached the head of the creek, Maw and Paw Lewis were waiting for me. These were truly "clever" people. It was a privilege to stay in their humble home. Maw was the best of mountain cooks, and I spent many a pleasant hour at her sumptuous table and sitting in a hickory bottom chair next to the warm grate listening to Paw's experiences and humorous stories. He wanted me to be accepted by the people and sometimes gave me needed advice. I had knelt on one knee in front of the old schoolhouse to pray and Paw took me aside and kindly said, "The Bible says, 'Every knee shall bow,' and we think you ought to pray on both knees." I gladly complied.

On one trip I could see by the twinkle in her eyes that Maw had a story she was a bustin' to tell me. It seems that a "Holy

Ma and Pa Lewis. I spent many an enjoyable night with
this dedicated Christian couple on Spring Creek.
They were like father and mother to me.

Roller" preacher, as folks called him, had come to preach one
night in the old schoolhouse. Several people came to hear him
along with Maw and Paw. As the preacher began to "Get under
the Power" he danced back and forth quoting the Apostle
Paul as saying that we should greet one another with a "Holy
Kiss". Maw said, "You know that preacher danced right by his
wife and kissed a young pretty woman on t'other side of her.
Believe you me, ifin I hada been his wife, I'd a got up and
knocked all the power outa him." Paw chewed a couple of
times, spit into the grate, and with a wry grin said, "She'd a
done it too!"

Once when I went to Spring Creek, I stayed with the Alvis
Smith family. Attendance had been poor. The Baptists and the
Holiness people and our people should work together, I felt,
for it was a small community. I wasn't sure I would be invited
back or not but took the text: "Naaman was a good man, but
he was a leper." (II Kings 5:1) I began pacing the floor in my
heavy boots and telling them they were good people but since

they couldn't worship together, they were sinners. The harder I preached, the happier they got. At the close they all came up and shook my hand, and on the way home with my host, Alvis said: "You know, I told Paw Lewis you were just a young feller and would have to larn to preach."

The news got around quickly and the next morning the old schoolhouse was almost full. I was "larnin'."

GOD'S COUNTRY

Returning from my Spring Creek appointment on a beautiful, sunny Sunday afternoon, the trail dropped quickly down a branch that widened into an ever-growing stream as other branches joined together. There were long stretches of trail winding through hardwood forests that once shaded Cherokee Indians. They had had a small village in one place. I found a spot where there were piles of flint chips and broken arrowheads where they had made their arrows. I even found a well-preserved stone axe almost completely buried beside the trail. So, as I rode under the giant trees, I gazed at the chestnut oaks that lined the ridges down past the red oaks and the white oaks, the scaley bark hickories, ash, black gum, to the beech and sycamores where water was more plentiful—each specie with its own distinctive shape. It was in these deep creek bottoms that pioneers found the logs for their cabins. For here were the groves of tulip poplars that grew so close together that they stood straight and slender, each one trying to reach higher than the other to bask in its upper branches in the sunlight that could not reach the bottom of the holler. I had much to enjoy of nature and much to wonder about as I rode and fantisized of what might have transpired when Indians, pioneers, and Civil War raiders traveled this very same trail. What a blessing to ride leisurely through such historic beauty, unspoiled by lumberman's axe or miner's pick and shovel.

CHAPTER VII

THE INITIATION TESTS

When on rare occasions a new family moves into an isolated community such as Jack's Creek, a period of initiation or testing must be gone through before being fully accepted. The designation of "Furriner" is hard to shake off. Learning local pronunciations, customs, and speech patterns helped a great deal. A woman snickered when I said, "Crick" for "Creek". She was right. But I had said "Crick" all my life in the West. We learned to say "holler" instead of "hollow", and "yaller"

View up Red Bird River
from Jack's Creek.

instead of "yellow". When asked how I was, to say, "Just common," instead of "I'm fine." My father came in for a visit one time and was caught completely off guard when a young widow he was talking to in the store said, as she was leaving: "Go home with me." Dad turned red and finally sputtered: "I guess I can't today." She and I laughed when we saw his embarrassment. All she was saying was "goodby". I answered in the proper fashion: "Cain't, stay with us." And she got on her mule and left still amused. Having the party in the parsonage and in many other ways we had shown our people we were "clever" or hospitable and not proud.

Postmaster Ruth knew we needed a cow. She had a little Jersey that had come fresh only a short time and so tried out my trading skills by making an offer. The price seemed a little high, but the cow looked good to me. Not knowing I was supposed to haggle, I accepted her price and paid her. The Jersey had always been milked while standing in an open stall with only a box of feed to keep her steady. Secondly, no one had ever told me that cows were never milked by men. Her name was Pied, and I led her home. She seemed very gentle. I had built a stanchion to hold her head and gave her some grain. I got a milk bucket, but Pied was not about to let a man milk her. She kicked, stepped in the bucket, and swatted me with her long tail. I fastened her tail to a wire from the ceiling and eliminated one hazard, but still had a long way to go. But with a lot of patience, we finally became friends and she got used to me. I had noticed some lumps in the milk from time to time and said to Ruth, "Pied seems to have mastitis." With a glint in her eye she replied. "Ifin you had asked me before you bought her I would have told you." I sent for some medicine and cured the mastitis and had a good cow after all. I later learned that Ruth was considered to be the best trader in that section of the hills.

I came out better on some of the other tests put to me. I walked into Darius' store at the mouth of Old House Branch

Ruth Roark and son Raymond.

one Saturday morning to find several young men sitting on the counter and sacks of feed next to the big old coal stove. Manford nudged Gilbert and said with a grin, "Hey, preacher, we've all shouldered that bag of coffee. How about you giving it a try?" In the center of the floor was a one hundred-fifty pound cloth sack of coffee beans. I knew I could lift that much weight, but the bag was bulky and my arms could not reach around it. Other men who had been whittlin' and swapping knives gathered around to watch the new preacher who was not about to back down. I thought I saw a way. So, squatting down, I worked all the beans out of the lower corner except a few to give me a good grip. Using the other arm to balance it, I raised the bag to one knee and then to my shoulder and stood up. The bag was too bulky to stay and slid down my back but I had stood up with it. Manford looked somewhat abashed and sliding off the counter said, "All right, boys, if the preacher can do it, I guess we can too."

Tennessee produced a Sergeant York, noted for his marksmanship and heroism. The Kentucky Hills have also provided some keen woodsmen and marksmen since the days of Daniel Boone. It was my privilege to get to share some of my skills with a few of them, before too long.

It was early spring and I was checking over my garden for plowing when I heard two dogs barking. Looking across the creek, there was a rabbit scurrying around the open hillside with the dogs in hot pursuit. Behind the dogs were two barefoot boys trying to keep up. The rabbit made a sharp turn and darted into a small brush pile at the foot of the hill. The dogs were not aware of this sudden turn and kept straight on. During the confusion of losing the scent, I had time to get my .22 caliber rifle with open rear sight and return. I had handled rifles and shotguns since I was twelve years old, but I had never killed a rabbit with a rifle while it was running; with a shotgun, yes. By the time the dogs had trailed back to the brush pile, which was about fifty yards from me, the boys had reached a vantage point to see what happened next. The rabbit darted from the brush pile full speed ahead. I raised the rifle and fired. The rabbit tumbled end-over-end. I was as surprised as the boys, but letting on as though it was easy, I called: "There's your rabbit, boys. Better get it before the dogs do." They grabbed their game and dashed for home. Word got around: "The preacher is a crack shot." So, I was accepted and the men invited me to compete with them. We drove nails into posts with bullets and lit matches at fifty feet. But chicken "shoots" were my downfall.

At chicken "shoots" you actually shot at the chicken. The first one to draw blood got the chicken. (Whoever heard of the Humane Society in the mountains?) The chickens were tied to a bush or stake about three hundred yards away on the hillside. You paid your quarter and took a shot. A boy hid behind a rock or log for safety and checked the chicken for blood after each shot. Elevation and windage had to be taken into account.

The best shots had to wait until the others had a chance. I have seen the same ones go home with as many as eight chickens tied together and slung across their saddles. I may have hit one or two, but I was accepted as one of the community at least for trying.

Two young men, cousins, on my Bowen's Creek Circuit, were considered the best squirrel hunters in the area. They spent a lot of time in the woods during hickory nut season. John, the younger, was the son of our Bowen's Creek Church leader. "Come over," George said, "and John will take you hunting." It was an easy invitation to accept. John's mother made the best biscuits and gravy around. She was up way before daylight, wrung a young chicken's neck and had it in the skillet before the biscuits were done. Add gravy, homemade sorghum molasses and black coffee and John and me were rarin' to go. And with our rifles, we headed for a holler where he had seen fresh hickory cuttings. John suddenly turned into Daniel Boone. He began slipping cautiously through a beech grove with me close behind. Dawn was just breaking. Here and there the little birds were waking with sleepy chirps. We stood like statues listening for another sound—the sifting of hickory or beech hulls down through the leaves. A squirrel would be working on an early morning breakfast.

Bertha Osborne and daughter
skinning a squirrel.

John turned very slowly and pointed to a smooth crotch high in a beech. In the dim morning light I could see something the size of a walnut sticking up on the back side of the crotch. As my eyes became accustomed to the dim light, I noticed a little bead of an eye watching us without moving. John very slowly raised his rifle and with careful aim squeezed the trigger. The rude "crack" of the rifle echoed and re-echoed through the holler and all nature sounds ceased. "You didn't get him," I said. "Let's go see," John answered in self-confidence. Sure enough, the squirrel lay in a heap on the other side of the tree. The bullet had gone right through its eye. "Saves meat to shoot through the head," John said. "I always shoot them in the head." After that exhibition of marksmanship, I let him do the shooting. I carried the squirrels. My, they were good the way his mother cooked them with gravy and dumplins! I was tested in many other ways, but will contribute only one more story to this chapter. A little psychology helped me with this one.

My predecessor had told me that the garden soil raised delicious watermelons, but the boys stole or destroyed them all, and it was no use to try. My father had told me something that worked when he was a boy so I was determined to try it out.

When the ground got warm enough, I sowed several hills of watermelons by the fence next to the road. I noticed the boys looking at the young melon vines as they developed. I would say to them as they came by: "If you like melons, looks like we may have some nice ones." What they didn't know, was that behind a couple of rows of tall Kentucky Wonder Beans, staked on poles, was another patch. But these were banana melons. They would ripen earlier than the watermelons and when fully ripe, put out the sweetest banana aroma that ever tickled your nostrils.

One day a couple of boys came by and stopped as usual to see how the watermelons were developing. I saw them sniffing the air. They had smelled a ripe banana melon. "Climb over the fence, boys, I've got something to show you." They hesitated but came. Once behind the bean patch they looked with wonder at the long yaller melons. I reached down and cut one open with my pocket knife and said: "Try it. I think you'll like it. Now, when the watermelons are ripe, we'll cut some of them too." I gave away a lot of melons to all the boys, but never had one stolen. It's no fun to steal something that is given to you. There were plenty of melons for all of us.

Jessie weeds Jack's Creek garden—1949
The new stone school replaced the old wood school
that burned by lightning.

CHAPTER VIII

CUNNING AND WIT

Outsiders sometimes picture our Kentucky Mountain people as poor, ignorant "hillbillies" with hot tempers, strange speech, or moonshiners who are continually feuding and fighting. Once you are worthy of being accepted among them, you soon learn that for the most part they are warm, hospitable ("clever"), proud, self-reliant, and full of humor and wit. I have enjoyed many a chuckle as a guest in their humble homes sitting by a glowing grate in the evening after a delicious meal, listening to stories they shared with me.

"Butter eye", "Black Joe", Slicky John", and "Fiddlin Jim" are a few nicknames they gave each other. Almost everyone was given a descriptive title. I finally begged Ruth to tell what my nickname was. "Square Jaws", she said with a twinkle. She never elaborated whether it was the shape of my face or my stubborn streak that earned me that name.

SLICKY JOHN had moved back to Jack's Creek and married one of our widows. He opened a small store and settled down to the good life and doing considerable preaching. In earlier days, he had run a small coffee shop in Hyden as a front to sell moonshine. He did so well evading the law in that dry county seat, he earned the name of "Slicky John". He laughed as he told me how lawmen would come into his shop to drink coffee at the counter. When a regular customer came in and sat down beside the sheriffs, John would say, "How about a coke?" and reaching into the refrigerator, would set a coke bottle on the counter.

The sheriffs were unaware that the coke bottle was filled with moonshine as they all drank and visited together. Slicky John may have inherited his cunning from his grandfather, "Fiddlin' Jim," whom he told me about.

Jack's Creek and "Slicky" John Sizemore department store. Naomi Nelson left; Jessie Plowman right. 1950

FIDDLIN' JIM

Slicky John loved to talk about his grandfather, Fiddlin' Jim, who lived during the Civil War days. Most mountain people were Republicans who supported Lincoln. So, Confederate Raiders had no qualms over stealing food and mounts when they passed through.

According to history, Raider John Hunt Morgan needed one thousand horses to supply his men and decided to make another raid into Kentucky to get them. It was his last.[1]

---

[1] Edison H. Thomas, *John Hunt Morgan and His Raiders,* p. 97.

The end of May, 1864, Morgan left Virginia with a column of men and crossed into Letcher County, Kentucky, through Pound Gap. As they spread out through the mountains, part of the column passed by Fiddlin' Jim's cabin while he was back on the ridge looking for some tasty young squirrels. When he got home in the afternoon, he found his cabin ransacked, and worst of all, his faithful bay mare stolen. He knew he could not get her back except by trickery. So Jim set his muzzle loader rifle in the corner, pulled his fiddle out of its hiding place, and started down the river after the Raiders. Soon he could see their campfires through the twilight—"The edge of dark." As he drew closer he could hear their laughter as they feasted on stolen food. Slipping past their sentries, Jim began playing lively tunes on his fiddle. The men clapped and encouraged him to play more. All the time he was moving from one campfire to another looking for his mare. Finally, he spotted her tethered with some other horses. Working his way around to the officers' tent, he played his best until the captain came out and thanked him for entertaining the men. "Anything I can do for you?" the Captain asked. "Wal, there is one little favor. One of your men took my bay mare, and I shore need her to work my crop." The Captain, being in a generous mood, called one of the men and told him to fetch Jim's mare for him. Jim thanked the Captain and rode his mare back up the river and home. He was feeling good. He had met the enemy and won the skirmish with his cunning.

A CROP WITHOUT SWEAT

McKinzie finished high school and married a mission teacher. He was a talented speaker and did well in politics, and was finally elected to the state legislature. "Why should I sweat to put in a crop when I can use my brain?" he thought. He hired nephews to do the planting and then came the hot weather and hoeing. The expression, "White-eyed from hoein'," came from the experience of being on the hillside so long in the hot sun that your eyes rolled back from exhaustion.

A corn crop was hoed out twice in summer then it was "laid by" until foddering time. In order to chop out the weeds and pull dirt around the corn you stood two rows below the top row with a short-handled hoe. The person on row No. 1 had to get ahead before the second person could start or he would be chopping No. 1's feet.

McKinzie hit on the idea of hiring slower help cheaper. He then hired one good fast hoer and paid him extra. McKinzie started the slower ones out first—rows one, two, three, and four then he started his fast hoer on row 5. To keep his bare feet from being chopped, No. 4 had to speed up causing a chain reaction on up the rows. McKinzie always got his corn laid by first, and everyone wondered how he did it.

†††††††

SECOND MILE SAM

"Second Mile Sam" was a hard-working man who, with the help of his family, always made a good crop of corn. Jake and his woman lived alone about a quarter of a mile up the branch from Sam. Jake only had his mule to feed and a couple of shoats to fatten besides meal for his table, so he didn't bother to raise a crop. Claiming he had a bad back, he let his woman raise a small truck garden. Sam knew Jake was about out of corn, but thought he would let him suffer a little before offering to help.

Early one night Sam thought he heard something down by his crib. Dressing quietly and picking up his gun, he slipped out to investigate. Sam could make out in the dim moonlight that it was Jake filling a sack of corn from the crib. Laying down his gun, Sam picked up an empty sack and hurried up the path to

Jake's house and quickly filled it with corn from Jake's crib. Waiting for Jake to pass without being seen, Sam hurried and emptied his sack back into his own crib. All night long this went on. Finally exhausted, Jake went to bed and Sam went home. Come daylight, Jake arose to feed his mule, proud of all the corn he would have in his crib to get him by until spring. "Sam won't even miss it out of his big crib," he thought. When he opened the crib door, Jake looked in dismay. There was no more corn there than when he started carrying it the night before. Jake scratched his head, afraid to guess what might have happened. In a few days Sam came up the branch with a big sack of corn and said, "I heered ye might be a bit low on corn, Jake, so I brung ye some to tide ye over a spell." Jake looked at Sam rather ashamed, but all he could say was, "Thank ye, Sam." That spring Jake was seen on the hill with his mule plowin' and plantin' corn. His back had apparently gotten better. Sam smiled to himself. He had taught Jake a lesson and still kept a friend.

Hillside plowing with
"jump" or "grasshopper" plow.

CHAPTER IX

PRECIOUS HAY: A THREE DAYS JOURNEY

Corn shucks and nubbins won't keep an active young riding mare sleek and healthy for long. Our creek bottoms were too small to raise much hay, and I needed some badly for Dixie. There was one place fifteen miles away if we could get a truck through.

Wholesale grocery trucks managed to bring supplies from Manchester about once a month in their big high dual wheel trucks. They brought in feed, but no hay. Storekeeper, Leonard, had a dual wheel stake bed he used when conditions were right. His teenage son did the driving. "I found a hundred bales of last year's soybean hay, Herman, if you are game to try and haul it from Queendale," I challenged him. Herman was always game for anything. "Sure, but the truck's down at Paps and we'll have to walk down there to get it," he replied.

Now, Pap was his grandfather, Manford, who, with his wife Nan, lived at Jack's Creek when we first arrived. Our Phyllis loved Nan and often ran across the little field to visit and play with the Diddlers Nan sometimes had. Nan loved to tell how Phyllis first looked at her kitchen range and said, "That's a qwar stove."

Manford and Nan moved down river where the roads were better and where there was a good place to store the truck. It was spring and the days were warm and the nights cool. Herman and I started walking in our shirtsleeves. The boy in me got us started looking for bullfrogs. We found a copperhead out sunning on a rotten log, and squirrels feasting on mullberries. It was a "fun" hike. Nan cooked us a good supper of cornbread, pork backbone, shuck beans, and fresh poke sallat.

Manford's youngest son, Junior, the "baby" had just married a very young teenage girl and they were living with Manford and Nan in the one room cabin. Manford confided with me that Junior wasn't able to support a wife but thought he had to have a "doll" to play with. So, being the "baby", they gave in and let them live there.

We sat by the grate as the evening was chilly. There were two beds and the women took the kerosene lamp into the lean-to kitchen while we undressed for bed by the light of the coal fire. I was next to the wall, then Herman and Manford. Junior slept in the other bed with his wife and Nan.

Before daylight, Nan was up and had wrung the head off a chicken, cleaned it, cut it up, fried it, made biscuits and gravy, and a pot of strong coffee. What a tantalizing smell to wake up to! We had prayer and ate the delicious breakfast. Herman went out to the shed and got the truck started, and the two of us headed on down the river. We had a better road here and soon traveled the remaining eight miles to the Queendale Ford Motor Company Complex. Mr. Queen, the superintendent, had been my host several times when I rode down on Dixie to conduct services at Big Creek. There was plenty of last year's hay left in the large company barn. When we finally got hold of the farm manager to help load the one hundred bales, it was noon and Mr. Queen graciously invited us to eat with him and some of the employees.

Herman decided that since we were so close to Manchester that we might as well go by the wholesale grocer and pick up a few items they needed at the store; then go home the route of the grocery trucks down Flat Creek and then five miles upriver home. But it got dark before we got to the river. No one told us that they were working on the road at Flat Creek. So, we drove right out on an axle deep fill of mud and stuck. In the mountains, you don't fret, but take life as it comes. So we settled down for morning to come and the road workers to pull us out. It was a chilly night for shirtsleeves. Herman ran the motor every hour to warm us up and we lunched on groceries for our supper and breakfast. The bulldozer finally came and pushed us on through the mud hole, and at last we headed up the river home. As the muddy road climbed fifty feet above the river in one place, the dual wheels slipped out of the ruts and we felt a lurch towards the river by the back end of the truck. We gingerly climbed out the high side and found that a small sapling was all that was holding the heavy truck from plunging down the steep bank into the river. We hastily took what rope we had holding the hay down, and tied the truck to a sturdy tree on the upper side.

The closest phone was a mile back at Flat Creek, so I started walking. Leonard said he would be right down with a team of big mules and block and tackle. So we waited until Leonard arrived. The upper tree made a good anchor to stretch the tackle to the truck. Leonard then tied the pully rope to the double tree and the mules leaned into the weight of the load. As Herman slowly inched the truck forward, the rear wheels were snubbed back into the road. At last, late afternoon of the third day and we were home. Two nights and three days to get one hundred bales of hay just fifteen miles away. What precious hay!

CHAPTER X

THE TRAGIC RABBIT HUNT

"HELP!" "HELP! Howard is shot!" This urgent cry was coming from high on the snow-covered hillside. Our Sunday morning service in the Jack's Creek schoolhouse had just been dismissed and we were coming out on the playground when the cry greeted our startled ears. Gilbert, high on the hill, was frantically waving and crying over and over, "Howard has been shot! Help me!"

Several men and boys hurried up the steep, slick hill to help. I ran to the phone and cranked out a short and two longs, our hospital number ten miles away to get Doc. All I could tell him was that a man had been shot. Doc was on his way on his motor rail car to Phillips Fork. I sent a boy with Dixie and a mule to meet him. Picking up a small axe, I too, started up the steep hill. The rescuers were on their way down. They had found Howard slumped beside a stump with a gaping wound in his abdomen. He had been standing on the stump watching for Gilbert to jump a rabbit. The butt of a sawed-off shotgun rested on the stump. It was an old gun with an external hammer and when he turned to see where Gilbert was, the gun slipped, hitting the hammer and discharging a full load of shot into his midsection.

The men were frantically trying to drag Howard down the hill, causing even faster internal bleeding. I asked them to lay him down and take off their jackets. Then to cut two saplings for poles to improvise a litter with the jackets buttoned around the poles. We laid Howard on the litter and wrapped more jackets around him. Gilbert was weeping. Howard was still conscious and praying with every breath, "O, God save me!" His voice was getting weaker.

Widow Phronie lived in a small cabin on the side of the hill, and she insisted we bring him in out of the cold and put him on her bed, even though he was bleeding badly. Phronie had some cotton that I pressed into the wound, but could not stop the internal bleeding. Howard was going fast and we were helpless to save him. Soon, all life was gone. I heard someone say, "You might as well ride up and head Doc off. We don't need him now."

The body was carried down to Howard's house next to the parsonage. I laid him out on a pingpong table I had made for the young people. Lena Mae kept asking me over and over: "Did he ask about me?" She and Howard had had a quarrel over his going rabbit hunting instead of to church with her. The only comfort I could give her was, "Lena Mae, he was praying." I always appreciated Jessie in times like these for her love and comfort to the bereaved. She was strength to Lena Mae.

The men had already started digging the grave and I picked a helper to make the coffin. As was the custom, I measured the body: 5'8" by 28". Poplar boards are soft and easy to work with and I soon had the coffin and outside box finished. We covered the coffin and lid with grey cloth, then I looked at the corpse that was outside on the table. The weather had warmed up. The late afternoon sun was shining on the body. To my horror the body was bloating and fluid was oozing all over the pingpong table. I ran into the house and called Doc. "Why did you turn back, Raymond? I'm in trouble." "You can handle it, Roscoe. Just stuff the hole with more cotton and tape as tight as you can to hold it in." I did this, then my helper and I struggled to lift the corpse over in the coffin. It wouldn't go in! "There isn't time to build a bigger coffin!" I said in desperation.

With all our weight pressing with both knees; first one side then the other we wedged the body to the bottom of the coffin. The abdomen still protruding an inch above the top of the coffin, I went for Lena Mae. "I've got to nail the lid down tight. There can be no viewing of the remains in this condition." She bravely looked at the now puffy face of her husband and turning away said, "Just do what you have to." I pressed the lid down, and we nailed it tight. There was no open casket at the wake that night, nor at the burial the next day. I played very little pingpong after that. The stain wouldn't wash off the table.

CHAPTER XI

CHRISTMAS TIME

Christmas is a special time anywhere for children and certainly no exception in our Red Bird River area. They enjoy portraying the Christmas story, singing Christmas carols, and reciting poems. The parents always come to the school programs to hear and watch their younguns. Many of the families had little to share with the children for Christmas. Our church people all over the United States made sure we had plenty of toys and candy for all of the children in our area. Just before Christmas, packages of toys and candy came pouring in to the Mission center and the out-stations as well. The mail carriers had extra work at Christmas bringing in the packages. It often took a string of three mules to bring in one day's shipment. The mail sacks hanging over the sides of the mules would drag through the water or get splashed on at the crossings. The bags were not waterproof, and we often had to dry out soggy dolls, games and candy. But every child got at least one real nice toy and a poke of candy. Usually there was enough candy for the parents as well.

One year we were short of enough candy to treat everyone. Beverly Center said they had plenty to share with us so I started early one morning on Dixie to cover the twenty mile round-trip before dark. Manford had removed Dixie's shoes and replaced them with ice cleated shoes and ice nails. These special shoes would bite into the icy trails and not slip. It was a beautiful cold day, but the trail and river crossings were frozen and treacherous.

Dixie had a chance to rest for awhile at the Beverly barn. I stripped her heavy Western saddle off and found an empty stall with hay in the rack. The boarding school boys took good care of the mules and horses. I was in time to have lunch and a short chat with some of the staff before picking up the coffee sacks of candy. One of the boys had Dixie saddled and waiting for me. We sewed the tops of the sacks together with nails and hung them over the saddle. I climbed on top and worked my feet back under the sacks into the stirrups. It was a heavy load even for Dixie's sturdy legs. She took right off. She was always ready to go home. I carefully guided her through the thirteen river fords to keep from getting the candy wet. We were almost to the mouth of Jack's Creek and though Dixie was very tired, she picked up her pace. But, alas, there was one more narrow embankment to climb to get to the Jack's Creek crossing. It was narrow and steep and icy. About fifteen feet above the river, one of the sacks hit an outcropping of rock, throwing Dixie off balance. Her front foot went over the side and she had no choice but to make a lunge for the gravel bar below. She landed flat on her side. I cleared her and fell on my hands and knees in the edge of the water. The candy was caught on a bush about halfway up the bank. I thanked God I wasn't hurt, then nearly sobbed as I looked at Dixie's lifeless form, stretched out, her eyes closed and not breathing. Dixie was almost a part of me. We spent many an hour together on the trail every week. I stepped over to her and loosed the cinch and tried to pull the saddle and blanket off her. The wooden stirrup was caught under her ribs, and I gave a hard jerk to free it. As I did, the motion started her heart and breathing. She sucked in air with a gasp and struggled to her feet. I was overjoyed. She stood there trembling. I walked around her, stroking her neck and sides and legs. There was a sore spot where she had landed on the stirrup, but apparently no fractures. She stood there breathing normally again and began nuzzling me as though to say, "Okay, let's get going. I want to get home." The blanket and saddle went back on, but loosely cinched. I retrieved the candy pokes and loaded them and finding a way to get back on the trail again, walked Dixie the rest of the way. Jessie knew something had happened when she saw me walking. Dixie got dry bedding, a good rub down and plenty of hay and grain that night.

Jessie, the two teachers, and I had to hurry to divide the candy into enough pokes to have one for each person who came to the program. The people came. Out of every branch and holler in the area, they came. Most of the men had revolvers stuck in their belts or high-powered rifles that they stood in the corners of the school room. The young fellows did considerable drinking at Christmas time as they do most places and sometimes got a little wild; so when I asked about the guns, one of the men said: "We just want to pertect ye ifin need be."

The program was a success. Once again we had had the privilege of seeing the excitement in the children's faces and the shy looks of gratitude from some of the "LEAST" ones. They were certainly worth the effort.

CHAPTER XII

MOUNTAIN PREACHERS AND PREACHING

"You preached a mess this morning," folks were saying as they greeted a minister friend of mine who was visiting us from the west. Fred gave me a puzzled look. "Was I that bad?" I laughed. "You were great. They liked the message so well they were comparing it with the mess of pottage Jacob cooked for Esau." "That's a new expression to me," Fred said.

Mountain preachers were very literal in their preaching. Some were unlearned. Some could not read or write. The King James version of the Bible, sometimes referred to as "St. James", was the only acceptable version. There were many varieities of doctrinal emphases. Some were Pentecostal or Holiness; often nicknamed "Holy Rollers". There were United Baptists, Missionary Baptists, and even Snake Handlers. Almost all baptized by immersion. Most of the many mountain preachers I learned to know, impressed me with their sincerity. The people watched our lives and if we did not live up to what we preached, we lost favor with them. Preachers were held in high esteem by all mountain folks. I have felt as much at home in a moonshiner's cabin as in any other home.

It took some time to break down the barriers some of the mountain preachers put up between us. First, they were afraid of my larnin'; secondly, I prepared many of my messages; and thirdly, I was receiving a salary for being there. Love and understanding was the only way I knew to break through this barrier. God, through His Spirit, directed me many a time, plus the help of my charming wife Jessie, whom they quickly learned to love.

Funerals and Memorials were "Preached" at the gravesite during the summer Sundays after corn was "Laid by." Every preacher was welcome to join in and every preacher was expected to be heard. I have participated at all day meetings with up to ten other preachers. This was a social time, as well as remembering family patriarchs and the ones who had died the past year. The family and neighbors where the memorial was held usually killed a shoat or a sheep to roast plus other food carried in. Horses and mules were traded and sometimes out of sight of the crowd, moonshine was drunk.

Five preachers leaving grave site
at the end of a memorial meeting.
1949

First Memorial Meeting

I was under the appointment of the Evangelical Church Mission Board. So my first Memorial Service turned out to be another time of testing for me. One of the leading mountain preachers had boasted he was going to preach me out of the country. The word got back to me, and learning that I was to speak after Shelby made me a little uneasy. The gathering was large. The day was sunny and warm. Our horses and mules were tethered under some scrub oaks over the side of the hill. It came Shelby's time to preach. He opened with the text: Acts 4:12. "There is none other name under heaven given among men, whereby we must be saved." He then began in a loud masterful voice to say that there was no such name in the Bible as "Evangelical": that preachers who were paid to preach were nothing but "Hirelings." To be rich and ride on a fat horse was a sin. I looked over the hill at the horses. Dixie was the only one sleek enough you couldn't hang your hat on her hipbone. Even the mule swappers heard and were gathering closer in. They wanted to hear what the new preacher would have to say about Shelby.

When my turn came, I stood up and walked out in front of the people. The situation was tense, but God had shown me what to say in the last few minutes. Peace and love had filled my heart. Using the same text that Shelby had used, I complimented him on his text and elaborated on the beauty and saving power of the name of Jesus. Shelby was deflated. The people settled back and the Spirit of God prevailed.

A Warm Coat For A Cold Ride

Preacher Shelby carried the mail twenty-eight miles round trip to Mill Creek each weekday. Winter came with its cold and snow. Shelby's route passed right in front of our house. I saw

him coming one cold morning. He had on an old ragged coat
and a shawl was tied around his head. Outside churches often
sent clothing in for us to give away to the needy. Jessie said,
"There is a warm, fur-lined coat that ought to fit Shelby."
"Great idea," I replied. "Why don't you take it out to him?"
Jessie ran out with the coat. Shelby was overwhelmed with
gratitude as he shed his old thin coat and put the warm one on,
pulling the collar around his ears as he rode off.

Taylor Sizemore, preacher and mail carrier,
headed for post office to start his mail route.

Spring came, beautiful as always in the hills. Dixie was a
fast-gaited mare and I caught up with Shelby at Spring Creek as
he was bringing in the mail. We "Howdied" and rode on together in awkward silence. Apparently our returning good for
his efforts to run us off was really bothering him. Finally, he
blurted out, "Preacher, you shore have got a fine woman." I
agreed, and we became more friendly as we rode on.

My Woman's Hurtin'

Before daylight one morning we heard someone calling under our bedroom window. It was Preacher Shelby. He was saying, "My old woman is hurtin' somethin' awful. She allus has a hard time. Can you get Doc to come quick?" "Doc's away," I replied. "You go home and boil some water and I'll go get Granny, and we'll be right there." Saddling Dixie and taking a flashlight to find the way, I rode up the river a mile and a half to the mouth of Asher's Fork. Steve Holland's fox hounds began baying as I came to the gate to call. Long, lanky Steve came to the door of the little cabin with a kerosene lamp in one hand and a gun in the other. "It's Preacher Plowman, Steve. I need Granny to go with me to Preacher Shelby's. His woman is having pains close together and we need to hurry." Steve got Granny up and saddled her mule while she dressed and got her bag that she kept packed for just such a call. We were soon on our way, splashing through the river and up Jack's Creek to Shepherds Branch. We were just in time. Granny delivered another member into Shelby's growing family. His woman was doing fine and Shelby thanked us both for coming.

The Fruit Of Love

After nearly four years at Jack's Creek, Jessie and I were called away to another appointment. Preacher Shelby heard about it and stopped at our gate to talk. "I heered ye are leavin' us?" "Yes, we must go where God leads," I replied. Reaching down from his horse, he grasped my hand in brotherly love. Tears were streaming down his leathery face. "I shore hate to see you go." This was the man who had told the community he would preach us out of the country.

††††††

MY LIVELIEST SERMON

I will never forget one memorial meetin' that was held at the head of Jack's Creek for one of the patriarchs who was buried there. Children and grandchildren who had found jobs outside the hills had all gathered back for this special occasion. It was a beautiful warm summer Sunday. Folks were riding in from all over. About six preachers were expected to come. I had preached at several memorials now, and felt more at home. I still didn't get as loud, or as excited as the ones who got "Under the Power".

Folks were sitting among and below the graves with the hand-carved head stones. I was the first to speak and stood just below the crowd. The horses and mules were tethered in the shade to my left as I faced my audience. There was a patch of brush to my right. Most of the young women were nursing their babies, and fanning flies away with small branches.

Memorial meeting, Upper Jack's Creek—1957.
Roscoe preaching.

I don't remember my text or what thought I tried to bring. I do remember that after I started, I happened to look down in time to see a small frightened harmless green-striped lizzard leaving the crowd and darting my way as I stood still. As it got closer, it saw the dark opening of my trouser leg above my shoe, and, thinking it looked like a safe place of refuge, darted up my leg. I had been almost hypnotized by the lizzard's quick movements and reacted too late. The lizzard stopped at my knee. I didn't want it to go any higher, so without losing my thought as I preached on, I began stomping hard to try to shake it loose. The congregation had not seen the lizzard. They thought the Mission preacher had finally "got under the power". They began getting blessed. As soon as I found a good stopping place, I turned the service over to the next preacher, and slipped into the brush on my right to check on that pesky little lizzard. That was the shortest and liveliest sermon I ever preached.

Uncle Johnny Napier at memorial meeting
on Upper Jack's Creek.

††††††

THE HOUND DOG SERMON

One of my perceptive mountain friends once said, "It ain't allus what you preach, but how you preach it that pleases many of our folks." One of our mountain preachers was so well-liked that folks would come for miles to hear him. One day a boy said to his father: "Paw, you talk so much about Preacher Sam. I'll bet I can preach as good as he can." "Hush your mouth, boy. You cain't preach and you know it." "I'll just show you, Paw." And he started off. "Last night I took old Yaller and old Blue up on the ridge to find us a fox trail. We hadn't gone fur when old Blue hit a trail. Offen they went.

Matt Shepherd and his hounds

Old Blue bawlin, 'Ow, Ow, Ow,' and old Yaller right behind him, 'Yi, Yi, Yi.' I hear them now a headin' up Paw's Branch, old Blue's still in front. 'Ow, Ow, Ow.' " The boy was getting excited now. "Thar they go over into Blue Hole and up Possum Branch. They're headed this a way now. I believe ole Yaller has got past old Blue and is out in front. Yes, I hear him, 'Yi, Yi, Yi.' But Blue won't quit. He's about to catch old Yaller again, 'Ow, Ow, Ow.' It's old Blue—It's old Yaller—It's old Blue— Now they're running neck and neck." The boy was gasping for breath at this point. The spellbound father jumped up and slapped the boy on the back and cried, Hallellujah, son, I didn't think you could do it."

††††††

THE SNAKE BIT PREACHER

There are some who believe that the Scripture that states, "They shall take up serpents," means that a person with enough faith can pick up a poisonous snake and it won't bite him. Timber rattlers and copperheads were the most common in our area. I had a good member who went to most of our meetings and if he saw a suspicious-looking box with air holes, he would say, "If you got snakes in the box, get them and go someplace else. We don't allow snakes in our meetins."

Timber rattler

Doc told me of a mail carrier preacher on Goose Creek who got in a big way while preaching and pulled out a big rattler. After a while, it bit him on the hand, and his arm began to swell. They rushed him to our hospital and Doc saved the arm.

"Are you going to handle snakes when you get well?" Doc asked. "I shore am," the preacher answered. "The reason I got bit this time was that while I was preachin' I got my eye on a pretty woman and the Devil took advantage of me and let the snake bite me."

††††††

THE ROOSTER SERMON

Preaching doctrinal sermons using seminary terminology has no place among our common people. Jesus spoke in parables, and I found that using everyday happenings as illustrations were of more lasting value.

I remember a hillside service one Sunday when Preacher Slicky John was to follow me. As I preached, I stated, "John has an old red rooster that stays around his store. And Betty has four white ducks. I was at the store one day, and a big rain shower came up sudden like, and John's old rooster was caught out in it. Before it could get under the shelter of the store porch, it was soaked to the skin. Its beautiful arched tail was all scraggly. It was the most miserable lookin' rooster you ever saw. About that time, here came Betty's four white ducks up from the creek, flipping their saucy tails, chattering to each other and happy as could be. The rain was running right off. What is the difference between the ducks and the old red rooster? It's the oil in the duck's feathers. The rain can't penetrate the oil. But the poor old rooster does not have that protection and he is miserable. You see, Christians are like that. The ones who have the Oil of the Holy Spirit are not bothered by the troubles that come. The ones without the Holy Spirit are completley drenched with trouble and are miserable."

I could see that John was excited. He couldn't wait for me to finish. So, I turned the service over to him. He jumped up and took off with this new revelation he had seen as I talked about his red rooster. And he preached one of the best sermons I had ever heard him preach. The parable, simple as it was, had touched John.

Six mountain preachers.
Slicky John Sizemore—extreme right.
Plowman—fourth from right.
Taylor Sizemore—extreme left.

CHAPTER XIII

BAPTIZINGS

Mountain people may differ in some of their doctrinal beliefs, but when they are baptized, they expect to be immersed. I have baptized over one hundred-fifty converts in the Kentucky mountains; all by immersion in mountain streams.

The saying is: "No one will get sick from being baptized regardless of the weather." I have baptized under all weather conditions, including breaking ice at the edge of the stream, and I have never known of sickness due to exposure, including myself.

††††††

THE ICY POOL

It was a raw winter Sunday that we gathered around a deep hole of water in Bowen's Creek. Icicles were hanging from the overhanging rocks. We had just completed a revival meeting and there were three teenage converts to be baptized. After singing, a scripture and prayer, I waded into the pool, breaking the thin sheet of ice along the edge. I sucked in my breath each step I took, until the water reached my hips. My legs soon became so numb that I didn't feel the cold anymore.

Martha, the eldest of the three girls, was waiting for me at the edge of the water. She was the niece of George, my faithful lay leader. I smiled reassuringly as I took her hand and led her into the deeper water. She kept her composure but the shock of each deeper step registered in her eyes. She stood almost waist deep in front of me. Beyond us was water over our heads.

Unnoticed by me, big George had waded out behind us just in case—Martha held a handkerchief over her mouth and nose, and gripped my left hand in hers. As I pushed her under the water, my right hand supported her shoulders to lift her out. The shock of total submersion was too much, and with a gasp and a lunge, we both lost our footing and headed into the deep water. Suddenly, an unseen hand lifted us to firm footing and shallow water. George had gripped his big hand through my trouser belt and saved us. George stayed with me for the next two candidates. They were brave enough to go through with it even after seeing what had happened to Martha. We sang another hymn and walked back to the warmth of the house and dry clothes.

George Napier and wife, Elsie, from Bowen's Creek.
My trusted layperson.

†††††

THE SANCTIFIED WALLET

George's son, John the marksman squirrel hunter, was converted in a Jack's Creek meeting along with several others. He decided to be baptized in Jack's Creek that Sunday afternoon at the close of the meetings.

Reverend Yoh had come in to visit from Ohio, and had offered to preach. He was quiet-mannered, and spoke in a low voice. I was sure he wasn't getting across to the people. In discussing it with George, his candid comment was: "He spoke loud enough for me." Reverend Yoh was getting some deep truth across where it was hitting home. The revival was a success and a large crowd gathered for the baptizing.

John's father and grandfather were dedicated Christians, both in speech and daily living. John was a young school boy, but he was not too young to know what he was doing. He kicked off his shoes and started to wade into the stream with me when a friend called to him: "John, your wallet is still in your hip pocket. Let me hold it for you so it won't get wet." John stopped and turned to say, "When I get baptized, my wallet gets baptized with me."

There wasn't much money in his wallet, then, but I am told that forty years later his wallet is still as sanctified as it was when it was baptized.

†††††

OUT OF BED, INTO THE WATER

It is about four or five miles from our Jack's Creek Center to the dividing ridge into Middle Fork. "A fur piece," as some would say. A widower lived in his log cabin on the Middle Fork side. Feared by his enemies in his younger days, Uncle Jim was still considered a "right mean" person even in his older years. He had few friends.

After his wife died, the children married and moved away except for his youngest daughter, Freda. She stayed to do his cooking and housekeeping. He could see, after a while, that Freda was getting restless and was wanting younger companionship. Uncle Jim was getting old and crippled and feared he would lose his housekeeper. He began giving permission for young men to call. Soon Freda became pregnant and had a baby.

Slicky John and I going to talk to Uncle Jim about baptizing. Freda waits for us.

Since Uncle Jim was getting a monthly food allowance under the Roosevelt Commodity Program, he also learned that they could now draw a monthly check for the child. He was glad to get the free food though he, like many others, didn't know what to do with some of the canned things they had "never heerd" of. Many claimed the cans of grapefruit juice "wasn't fit to drink," and "shore made pore gravy."

Freda had more babies over the years and their income had increased considerably.

But now Uncle Jim was bedfast and worrying about his past. He was conscience-stricken and wanted to talk to a preacher and confess his sins and become a Christian. The trouble was, he couldn't think of a preacher he felt he could trust. Someone mentioned the Jack's Creek Mission preacher. And one day a rider came with a message for me from Uncle Jim. "Would you come over and pray with me?"

On short trips, Jessie sometimes rode side-saddle on Dixie with me. But this was too long and rough a trail for her to go. So I said to her, "I guess I'd better saddle up Dixie and get on my way or it will be dark before I can get back." Jessie had a look in her eye that stopped me. "Isn't that where Freda lives?" "Yes, of course. She keeps house for Uncle Jim," I replied. "Why?" "I hear she keeps house for a few others, too," Jessie replied rather crisply. "I suggest you go down and get preacher Slicky John to go with you." I got the message and so eased off down to Old House Branch and John's store.

"Uncle Jim sent a message that he wants me to come over and pray with him, John," I said as I sat down on a bag of coffee beans. "Would you like to go with me?" I watched John's face as he studied me. The part Cherokee Indian blood was prominent in his large curved nose and high cheek bones, his deep dark eyes, and his broad brow. With a feather bonnet, he would look like a noble chief. We didn't always agree, but I loved this man and his charming wife, Betty. Finally, instinctively, he knew why I had asked. In his deep bass voice, he replied with a humorous glitter in those dark eyes, "Shore will; first thing in the morning. Betty can mind the store."

We left as soon as we had breakfast the next day and after two hours of hard riding, tied our mounts at Uncle Jim's gate. Freda and two or three of her brood met us. She scolded several mean looking hounds, shooed some chickens off the porch and led us into the dark interior of the log cabin where we could dimly see Uncle Jim lying in bed in the corner. He knew John and they greeted and shook hands and I introduced myself. He reached up his hand for mine and said, "I've heard of ye. Glad ye would come."

We visited. Freda poured some real black coffee from the pot on the old wood range, and brought a plate of biscuits. After the lunch, I took my Bible and began reading appropriate passages. Uncle Jim said, "I've been a pretty mean man in my day." John answered, "You know my past was pretty rough and God forgave me." We prayed and Uncle Jim said, "I believe." He had a different look in his face, like a load had been lifted. "I want to be baptized Sunday," he said. "How?" we asked. "There are plenty of strong young men around here that can carry me on a litter to Middle Fork," he replied. I looked at the inquisitive faces of the younguns peering at us from behind Freda's skirts and replied, "Yes, I guess so." John said, "We'll meet you at the Middle Fork baptizing hole Sunday afternoon." Uncle Jim said, "Take the night," "Cain't," we answered. "Go home with us." And we headed through chickens and dogs to the gate, thanking Freda for the coffee and biscuits. When we got home, Betty said, "Well, I see ye got back alright," and chuckled. Jessie wanted to know what success we had. "It was a profitable day. I look forward to the events of Sunday," I told her.

Word gets around quickly in the mountains. Hearing Uncle Jim had "Jined the church" brought out a big crowd for the baptizing. We sang old songs, "Shall We Gather at the River" and "Will the Circle be Unbroken," then we read scripture and prayed. Simpson was a heavy man, but two strong fellows picked up the litter and carried him over the gravel bar and into the stream until he was just a few inches above the water. John put his arms under Uncle Jim's shoulders. I reached under his hips. Another man held his feet. As we lifted Uncle Jim out of the litter, I repeated in a loud voice: "I baptize thee in the name of the Father, and of the Son, and of the Holy Ghost."

Then we lowered him under the water together and raised him back on the litter, held by the two young men. Another rough mountain man had turned to God and joined the great family of Christians.

CHAPTER XIV

DOC'S HELPER

THE TRACHEOTOMY

Raymond and I became close friends even though we were ten miles apart. I would relay the life signs on the phone for sick or injured patients, and he would tell me what to do or what medicine to give. I remember when old Manford had pneumonia. Sulfathiazol was a new "wonder" drug. Raymond had prescribed a certain dosage and then warned me to watch Manford's eyes. "If they start to get yellow, stop the medication." Sure enough, the second or third day, the whites of his eyes began to look jaundiced so I stopped the sulfa. This is the way we worked together.

About once a month, Raymond would try to get away from the pressure of the hospital and ride Maud down to stay with us at night, just to relax. Sometimes we would gig for frogs, or go fishing in the river or shoot my old muzzle loader rifle.

One of these evenings we were sitting at the supper table when a knocking was heard at the clinic door. It was young Manford. Dale, his two-year-old son was very sick. It was a short walk to the house. Dale was pale and listless, and breathing with difficulty. Raymond, suspecting the possibility of diptheria, looked at his throat, but could see no membrane forming. So he left some medication and returned to the house with the understanding that we would check again later. Manford was back in an hour. Dale was worse. This time a membrane was showing. Doc said, "If I only had my surgical bag. I'll have to get it." The nurses had it ready for him when he arrived at Phillips Fork. They had sent it on the rail car by a member of the staff. Nearly two hours had elapsed when we returned to Manford's house. Little Dale was unconscious and turning blue. The kitchen table and a kerosene lamp became the operating theater. Manford and his wife were sent into another room. Ruth put Dale on the table and held his little blond head in her work-worn hands. I held his limp little body between my arms. Doc plunged the scalpel into Dale's trachea. Blood oozed. Doc inserted a tube and the oxygen-starved lungs sucked in clean fresh air and expelled the old. Like watching a miracle unfold, color came back. The blue cheeks became pink again and Dale opened his eyes. He could not speak or cry as the air flow was diverted from his vocal cords. Doc wiped the blood from his little throat and taped some clean gauze around the tube. The mother and father were called back in. Manford took one look at his live son and fainted dead away on the kitchen floor. So Doc had to revive him. Doc showed them the simple process of cleaning the tube that he fit into the other tube. Mucous and phlegm would clog it from time to time. Doc left for the hospital as medicine had to be ordered to fight the diptheria. Soon Manford was knocking on my door again. The tube was stopping up and they were afraid to touch it. So, I went back and cleaned the tube for them, then slept on the floor behind the stove so I could be near each time it needed cleaning. Dale and I became real good buddies the next two or three days. Finally the tube could come out and the hole repaired. We had to teach Dale to use his vocal chords all over again. Finally he could say, "Hello, Mr. Plowman," in a loud voice instead of a whisper.

††††††

THE AUTOPSY

Raymond was staying over with us another time when someone came to the door while we were eating breakfast. "Would Doc please come down Redbird River about a mile where a man is very sick?" We saddled and rode hurriedly, but when we arrived the man was dead. Doc checked him over and noticed capillary breakdown on the skin of his hands, arms, and body. So he began asking if anyone had noticed any ticks anywhere. Doc said the symptoms were similar to those of Rocky Mountain Spotted Fever, a dread disease often carried by ticks.

He then asked for permission in writing to open the abdomen and collect specimens of organs to send to the lab. The people left the cabin room and I held two small glass jars for Raymond as he began to cut. "I need a piece of liver. Ah, there it is. Now, a piece of spleen. Okay, that ought to do it." I sealed the jars while he sewed the abdominal wall together again. One of the women drew water from the well and poured some in a wash pan so we could scrub ourselves of any contamination. They were told to go ahead with the burial.

We arrived back at Jack's Creek in time for lunch. Jessie had it all set out for us. We gave thanks and Raymond began to fill his plate saying, "This sure looks good. I'm hungry." I put some spleen and some human liver on my plate (that's what it looked like to me), turned green and excused myself. Raymond laughed and said: "What's the matter, Roscoe, aren't you hungry?" I felt more like eating at supper time. The lab reports came back that the man died of typhus, a related disease to the spotted fever.

††††††

KILT STONE DEAD

I learned a great deal from Raymond as I worked with him,

or treated people as he directed by phone. Everyone came to us with their first-aid needs and medical problems. What we couldn't handle, we called Doc and followed his instructions.

One day old Joe, who lived up the creek a piece, came riding his mule in a big hurry. His grey hair was matted with blood and streaks of blood had run down his face and neck. Joe was wan, and fright showed in his pale blue eyes. He was almost crying when I got him off his mule and inside the clinic door. Jessie tried to calm him and began washing the blood with warm water. A large gash in his scalp had to be cleaned and shaved. Joe was really frightened and kept rambling, "I've been kilt stone dead." I taped the gash together and assured him he would be okay.

Joe told us what had happened finally. He and his wife, Katherine, lived in a board house beyond the Roark Post Office. A daughter and son-in-law were living with them for awhile. Joe had a quick temper and according to Joe he and his son-in-law had got into an argument that ended in a rock fight. Joe stopped to pick up a rock from the creek bed and the son-in-law ran out on the foot log and smashed Joe on the head. Fortunately, Joe was not knocked out and was able to get to us even though somewhat dazed.

Joe couldn't read or write and always came to me when he needed legal help. I notorized all his papers. He signed his name by touching the pen as I marked an "X", then Jessie and a teacher signed as witnesses. Joe was always intrigued by my shelves of books. He asked: "Do you read all them books?" When I answered in the affirmative, he replied, "My, you are a larned man."

Joe was afraid of prowlers and always kept his gun handy at the house. One night, the yard gate was accidently left open and Ben, Joe's mule, came in. Joe heard a sound in the shrubs near the house, so he got his gun and called out of the doorway, "That you, Ben?" Since Ben didn't answer, but started toward the familiar voice, Joe fired and poor Ben was mortally wounded.

CHAPTER XV

LOST IN MOONSHINE COUNTRY

The Mill Creek Church women wished to make some quilts that winter. So, instead of riding my usual route to Mill Creek, I headed for the mission center of Beverly. Here I picked up two coffee sacks crammed full of quilt scraps.

The route to Mill Creek from Beverly was via Blue Hole Creek. I had been that way only once before. Blue Hole was a beautiful stream, winter or any season. The trail winds through high cliffs, by rushing water in places, and deep, clear, blue-green pools that gave the creek its name.

About two inches of new snow had fallen and there were only a few tracks of travelers. Finally, in the late afternoon, we came to a fork in the trail. The only tracks took the left fork, but Dixie wanted to take the right. She had been over all these trails before I owned her, and I should have let her go. But reason said, "Follow the tracks." Dixie obeyed the rein reluctantly and we turned left.

Through the leafless trees ahead, a small cabin was picturesquly sitting against a backdrop of rising terrain covered with a grove of young tulip poplars standing like grey ghosts in the evening light. The lean-to porch was filled with people, but by the time we arrived, the porch was empty. Why had everyone gone? Then I remembered being told this was active moonshine country. Revenuers were not welcome here. Any stranger was looked upon with suspicion. I had a strange load of bulging coffee sacks and had never been this way before.

Not daring to approach the cabin any closer than the paling gate, I called: "Hello! Anybody home?" Immediately a raw-boned middle-aged man dressed in heavy boots, overalls, dark jacket and black slouch hat, stepped out on the porch. What instantly caught my eye was the high-powered lever action rifle he held in his hand. "Who air ye? What do ye want?" came his query. "I'm Preacher Plowman from Jack's Creek on my way to Mill Creek. I must have taken the wrong branch. Can you help me?"

All ages of children and adults began filling the porch. "Preacher" was a magic password in the mountains, besides most people knew Dixie's bay color and long blaze. The tense situation had suddenly relaxed and the man replied, "I heered about ye. Come in and take the night." It was the edge of dark, but I did some quick calculating. A cabin that size usually had two rooms and four beds. There were about twenty people to divide among the beds. "Thank ye," I replied. "They are looking for me and these quilt scraps at Mill Creek tonight. Can I get over to the Goose Creek road from here?" "Jest take the trail up the holler and ye'll cross over into Indian Branch and the Goose Creek road." "Thank ye," I replied. "Go with me." "Cain't. You come." And we headed up through the poplar grove to the ridge. Dixie seemed to know the way again and I gave her rein. The "edge of dark" had become night, and as we crested the ridge, Dixie stopped and wouldn't budge. Through the dusky shadows I made out a big mule head to head with Dixie. A deep voice came out of the darkness; "Who air ye?" I answered as I had at the moonshiner's cabin and the voice replied, "Oh, I heered of ye. I live jest over in the holler. Come take the night with me." "Cain't. You come." And we squeezed by and Dixie headed down Indian Branch for Goose Creek road and finally Mill Creek. The Hubbards were waiting and a little worried. Dave helped me unload the quilt scraps and feed Dixie at the barn. I patted her on the neck and thought, "You are a prize, old girl. I don't know what I'd do without you."

Pearl warmed up left-over corn bread, fried a piece of pork shoulder and poured a cup of black coffee for me. "Boy, this shore hits the spot," I remarked. Dave smiled. He had a kindly wrinkled face with sad eyes. Dave had suffered shellshock during World War I and was under daily medication. He was able to function well and ran one of the largest country stores in the area. Pearl was postmaster and helped in the store. Besides a large variety of food items, you could find anything from gun powder and caps, harness and turning plows to shoes and petticoats. The Hubbards were staunch Christian leaders in our church, and their home was always a haven for me. These were truly "clever" people and an enjoyable place to be after a long, hard day in the saddle.

Paling gate and fence.
Old House Branch at Jack's Creek.

CHAPTER XVI

DAILY RISKS, SOME DANGERS, A FEW DISCOMFORTS

Living anywhere in this great country of ours has its own particular risks, dangers, and discomforts. So, we found them in the Kentucky hills as well. However, these were peculiar to the area at a particular time period in history. We accepted the risks, dangers, and discomforts as a part of daily living. When I rode off on Dixie, Jessie would say, "I'll look for you when I see you coming." We knew we were in God's hands and, like our mountain neighbors, lived one day at a time.

I stayed overnight with moonshiners and bootleggers, without a fear. As a preacher I learned I was always welcome in any home, no matter how poor or well-to-do. We were living in "clever" country. The greatest hazards were the natural elements and pioneer conditions. Poisonous snakes such as copperheads, timber rattlers, and water moccasins struck at me many times. Dixie jumped and fell with me at least twice nearly crushing my foot. The tree climbers slipped several times as I was working on the phone line in high trees, and I fell twenty feet, taking bark and skin off as I slid to the bottom. Dixie and I were washed down the river once trying to cross in a "tide," but Dixie was young and strong and regained her footing and pulled us both out.

††††††

BLACK JOE

Black Joe was a bootlegger from Middle Fork with a mean reputation. Most people warned me not to cross him, but when he came and stopped at the house across the creek from our school with saddle pockets bulging and heavy, I decided I would have to confront him. Other young men, who enjoyed their weekend drinking, began to gather around the barn. So, I crossed the creek and walked in among them. They acted very nervous and had little to say. Black Joe had tied his horse to the paling. He was a fearsome-looking person, rugged, well-built, naturally dark complexion, with a slouch hat and a big revolver stuck behind his trousers belt.

I had second thoughts, but had come too far to back out now. I nodded to Joe and asked him if he would step around the barn for a talk. He complied as the others looked on uneasily. "Joe, some folks say you are bringing moonshine over here, and so I have come to you to ask that if you are, to please not sell it around our school." Joe's voice was soft and glib. "Mr. Plowman, someone is lying about me. I shore wouldn't do something like that. If you feel thata way, I won't come over here anymore. Just come and look in my saddle pockets and see for yourself." I was tempted, but the gun in his belt, and an inner voice, warned me not to do it. "No, Joe, I'll take your word. I just don't want moonshine around our school, so I thought I should check it out." We shook hands and I left.

The whole group soon moved down the creek to another barn. I never saw Black Joe in the area again. I did talk to one of the boys in the post office the next day. He said: "You were shore in danger. Ifin you had looked in those saddle pockets, Joe might have shot you. They were full of jars of moonshine."

††††††

MOONSHINE, POLITICS, AND FLEAS

Other bootleggers heard how I had confronted Black Joe, so they kept a respectable distance from our school. Politics is a big thing in the mountains; especially county politics. The big races were for sheriff, county judge, and jailor. Quite often eight or ten candidates would run for jailor. Usually the one who had the most kinfolks won. But it was a big event when candidates came to Jack's Creek to speak. Crowds rode in on an assortment of horses, mules, and even one ox with saddle.

Gathering for a political speaking

The bootleggers had a big day and we were fortunate if someone didn't get drunk enough to do a little wild shooting. There was an old, abandoned hog shed below the store where the speaking was to be. So, one of the bootleggers moved into it to dispense his wares. The creek had washed around the shed, cutting a new channel and isolating it from being used lately. Fleas had multiplied by hundreds and were in the rotten logs and dust and were starved. I became more interested in what I saw happening at the shed than in the speaking. Men were going to buy their supply of moonshine and returning covered with fleas, and were wildly scratching—certainly an amusing sight.

††††††

BEDBUGS—A NIGHT OF UNREST

Most mountain homes were extremely clean, regardless of their state of poverty. Head lice and bedbugs were a problem with a few. My predecessor had stayed in many of the homes and gave me a list of places to avoid if possible. One such home on the bug list was in the Spring Creek area. The family attended my services some, especially two of the boys that I was encouraging. So, when they kept begging for me to "Take the night" with them, I finally agreed on a warm summer day to "Go home with them."

When I got to the cabin and put Dixie in a stall, I dropped my saddle bags on the front porch. I had had experience with bedbugs before, and my nose picked up their peculiar odor when I entered the cabin. We had a good supper and fellowship. The folks were "clever" and wanted me to have their best. I certainly didn't want to offend them. We sat and talked as long as I could keep them up, but finally had to go to bed. The boys and I were assigned to one of the two rooms. There were two beds. The night was warm. I pulled a light cover over me and tried to sleep. But the army that attacked me was too much. I looked over at the other bed. The boys were sleeping soundly, unaware of the friendly little critters feasting on their blood. I finally threw off the cover so they could work on one side at a time. It was a long night. At home, Jessie and I went through all my clothes outside the house seam by seam. I'm sure the sacrifice was worth the good will of the family.

CHAPTER XVII

A GROUNDHOG AND MACHINE GUNS

I believe it was Steve Holland who shared an experience he had had while working the mines in Harlan. Since it happened about 46 years ago, I hope I can recount with some accuracy what he or one of his brothers told me.

Trouble had been brewing between union and non-union coal miners in the Harlan area. It was so serious that the governor had sent a unit of the National Guard with trucks and machine guns to keep the peace. They were there, in fact, when we arrived in 1937.

Steve had moved to Harlan but when the mines closed, he was out of work. He soon was short of cash and needed food. Suddenly he remembered seeing a groundhog hole up on the ridge. He took his rifle and slipped up on the ridge and laid down behind a log and watched for a groundhog to come out. The guard encampment was in the valley below. There were trucks with machine guns mounted on them. Steve had no idea of what was about to happen.

He laid very still and watched the hole. After awhile, a groundhog cautiously poked its head out and looked around. It finally decided all was well and climbed up to get a better view of the valley. Steve inched his rifle across the log, took careful aim and fired. Before he could get up to get his prize, the hillside was sprayed with machine gun bullets.

Steve was pinned down and didn't dare move. Finally he heard voices and an order to stand up slowly. He was surrounded with uniformed men and guns. "Why are you shooting at us?" an officer asked. "I warn't shooting at you," Steve answered. "I shot a groundhog for my family to eat." Where is it?" they asked. "It should be over by hit's hole," Steve countered. One of the men went over and looked and picked up the very dead groundhog. The tension eased and they laughed.

"Take your game and your gun and go home," the officer said. But warned, "No more shooting around here." Steve and his family ate the groundhog and then decided they better come back to Red Bird River. After Steve related his harrowing experience to me he remarked, "I shore am glad I'm a good shot."

CHAPTER XVIII

SHORT TALES—SNAKES AND OTHER EXPERIENCES

"SNAKE!" The yell came from behind me as my foot was descending on a fat copperhead sunning on our stone walk. I leaped on over it in time to avoid its poisonous bite. Jessie had saved me from a trip to the hospital.

JAR FLY?

I rode Dixie to my appointments. Jessie and the mission teachers walked to theirs; Sunday School, three miles to Upper Jack's Creek, daily Vacation Bible School, seven miles over the ridge to Bowen's Creek. Jessie and Shelly climbed the steep trail out of Bowen's Creek to the ridge top. Too tired to take another step, they stood and viewed the beautiful green panorama of Jack's Creek valley below. Shelly said, "That jar fly is buzzing awfully loud and close." Jessie looked down. At their feet a big timber rattler was coiled, shaking its rattles and prepared to strike. "SNAKE!" Jessie yelled and they jumped and ran most of the way home. The rattler missed. Adrenalin can do wonders for tired legs.

SAVED BY A NOSE

Dixie reared in the trail and almost threw me. I calmed her and dismounted and tied her to a tree. Just out of sight was one of the largest timber rattlers I have seen, lying in the trail. Dixie's keen nose had detected it just in time.

††††††

LEGEND OF THE VIPER

I had heard of vipers in the area and one day saw one sunning beside the trail. Dismounting, I took my riding crop and poked it. Instead of gliding away, it opened its jaws to one hundred and eighty degrees. This was something that had been told me, but hard to believe. It never got its jaws back together again the thirty minutes I watched. Mountain people believe that this is the viper that bit the Apostle Paul as he put sticks on the fire, and that God cursed it so it could never bite another human being. It may have returned to normal after I was out of sight. I'll never know. Ruth assured me later that it never could close its jaws again.

††††††

DANCING DIXIE

Dixie began dancing with all four feet in one place in the trail without music. "What in the world is going on?" I wondered since I was a part of the act. The answer was under her feet as she high-stepped to trample a copperhead before it struck her. She won without a scratch, leaving a mangled snake still twisting behind her as we rode on.

††††††

DON'T WEAR "SLIPPERS" IN THE GRASS

Boots were important to wear in the field when repairing the phone line. This time I was in a hurry. Tying climbers and repair wire to the pommel of the saddle and buckling on my tool belt, I mounted Dixie without changing from slippers to boots. We rode along the lines for three or four miles; no insulators broken, no lines down. It was a lovely day to ride in the sun and enjoy nature. The lines left the trail in one place and took a shortcut across a fenced field. This necessitated tying Dixie and walking several hundred yards. I saw a flash of copper at my feet and instinctively jumped high. A copperhead barely grazed my low cut shoe. A copperhead never gives warning before striking like a rattlesnake. No "slippers" in the field for me after that experience.

†††††

WATER MOCCASIN

A big bullfrog stared hypnotically into the beam of my flashlight as I raised my gig to add another frog to my string. My pants were rolled to my knees as I waded the cool water of Red Bird River. There were a lot of ordinary water snakes that usually swam away, but one was coming towards me unafraid. It had a wider head with poison sacs. I whirled, the frog jumped, I gigged the snake instead. It was my first water moccasin.

†††††

THE BAPTIZING MULE

Visitors who came to Red Bird Mission needed transportation from the end of the train line on Straight Creek. "Hospital Jim," as we called him, was a small, middle-aged man, disfigured with a mass of warts, but was pleasant, well-liked, and a hard worker. His life had been saved by our doctor at one time, and since he had no home of his own, the mission paid and boarded him to do odd jobs and run errands. It was Jim's responsibility to go after the visitors with the mission mules. He would take two boarding schoolboys with him. The long muleback ride over the mountain was quite an experience for some of the visitors from the city.

The schoolboys always looked forward to these trips in the summer, for they had one special mule they always took. Old Mike was the gentlest, most easy-going mule in the string, except for one fault. The boys would look over the visitors for the youngest, or most timid-looking woman in the group and put her on Mike. He was the best and safest trail mule we had. But when they came to the first deep river crossing near mission headquarters, Mike would stop in the middle of the river and refuse to go. Then, deliberately and slowly, admist the shrieks of the rider, would lie down and roll. The boys, of course, would rescue the fair lady. It was a hilarious time for them. It was worth the work of the trip just to get to play the joke. I think Jim enjoyed it as much as they.

†††††

THE CORNCOB PIPE

Mary, our next-door neighbor, wasn't old, but her face was getting wrinkled and leathery from working in the sun many years. She always wore the same old grey sunbonnet, and when she didn't have a chaw of her homecured "backy" in her mouth, a corncob pipe would be gripped in her tobacco-stained teeth. Only one married daughter was living with her and Darius. A man never gets the wood for the cookstove and Mary would be out in front of her house every day in her bonnet, the corncob pipe gripped firmly in her teeth, and swinging the axe with great energy.

Many mountain women chawed or enjoyed a cob pipe. Mary didn't know I was aware that she smoked and was afraid I might disapprove. So, every time she saw me coming, she would hide the pipe. I made a point to catch her in front of the house splitting wood and would walk down to visit a few moments. She would stuff the burning hot pipe into her apron pocket and pass the time of day. All the time, the curl of smoke was drifting up from her pocket. Finally, before it got too hot, much to her relief, I would move on.

My conscience began plaguing me as Mary was such a pleasant, kindly and generous person. So I walked up to her and, putting my arm around her shoulders, said, "Mary, why don't you get that pipe out of your pocket and smoke it before it burns you up. I've just been teasing you by coming by when you are smoking." "You young rascal! I suspicioned ye might be up to somethin' like that." She grinned and reached in her pocket and pulled out the pipe. I never told her that my great-grandmother who was born in Virginia loved her pipe too.

†††††

THE "WHUPPED" CHILD

Screams of a terrified child up the creek ahead caused me to spur Dixie to see what was wrong. What I saw was most amusing.

A woman, old enough to begin to show the lines in her hands and face of hard work and family cares, a rag tied around her head to keep her dark hair away from her face, as she had been leaning over scrubbing and beating clothes on a rock in the edge of the stream to clean them, was climbing up the bank with a big stick in her hand and beating it against the ground and yelling, in a fit of anger, "I'll whup you all the way to the house!"

Whatever the youngun had done to stir such wrath, he was

thoroughly frightened and squalled every step he made as he scrambled for the cabin above the road. For all the racket, he had not been touched by the stick.

I have never seen a child whipped by mountain parents. Grandparents will say, "Don't you dare touch that youngun!"

†††††††

YOUNG CASUALTIES

Many mountain homes were built of single-thickness inch boards; battened on the outside and papered with newspapers and catalog pages on the inside. They were cold in winter and the family crowded near the coal grate to keep warm.

Little blond Shirley picked up the "least one" that was fretting and began swinging it in her arms as she backed up to the grate to get warm. Ma was in the kitchen preparing supper and Pa was feeding the shoats. Shirley's skirts hung over the coals and flared up. Shirley screamed, dropped the baby, and ran out the door. Before her Pa could catch her and smother the fire, the dress had enveloped her in flames and burned off her blistered little body and face. The father bundled her up and rushed her to the hospital on his mule, but it was too late. Sweet little Shirley died. There were many burn casualties among children in winter. Our teachers warned of dangers of open grates and instructed on how to smother fire and not panic. Still there were casualties.

†††††††

A GENEROUS WOMAN

He was a ladies' man, I was told. I often saw him riding his mule loaded with coffee sacks full of used clothing to distribute to the widows and women that he visited from time to time. The incredible part was his woman. She waited at the post office and watched for the packages coming to the mission and copied off the name of the sender and the return address. Taking her list home, she would sit down, and in her own handwriting, tell a most pitiful story of poverty and need which she mailed to the unsuspecting gullible people and churches who mailed us clothing and toys for the mission to distribute.

Some of the people were wary enough that they mailed these letters to me for verification. I would have to say they were ingeniously written, and pulled at the heart strings. In spite of our warnings in our church publications, outside folks kept sending clothing and other goodies directly to this woman. Soon, she was getting almost as much as our local Mission Center. With so much to choose from for herself, she didn't need to wash what she was tired of, and used the castaways for rags.

It didn't seem to bother her to share her man with other women and ever so often she sent him off loaded down with clothing and other goodies to take to his "ladies" in other hollers. "What a generous woman," I thought, as I saw him starting off with another load.

††††††

SHUCK BEANS OR CHICKEN?

Johnnie Napier was a grand old man I soon learned to respect. He was white-headed with a white bristly mustache, except for the amber-stained fringes above his kindly mouth. He wore faded bib overalls over his generous chest, whether at work or at church. The only difference was that his church overalls were clean to start a new week.

Johnnie lived on Bowen's Creek in a good frame, two story home, and ran a steam-powered sawmill. His son-in-law Willie, and wife Bertha, and several nearly-grown grandchildren lived with him. Saturday was meal grindin' day, when neighbors rode in with corn across the saddle to wait their turn for the big stone burs to grind out the meal just the right speed to keep it from getting too warm and spoil the flavor. Johnnie was an expert and from time to time he reached his big hand into the bin to feel if the flour was the right texture and coolness.

No one in that household worked on Sundays other than feed, milk, and cook. I remember the first time Jessie and I were invited to Sunday dinner. When we were called to sit down at the table, without realizing the custom, Jessie sat next to me. There were only enough places for the men, and I whispered to her, "The women and children wait until the men have finished." She dutifully got up and joined the women in the kitchen. The table was loaded with wonderful food. A platter in front of me was heaped with beautifully browned fried chicken. No one passed food unless someone asked for it. I helped myself along with the others; first taking some shuck beans, cornbread, and salat. Finally, I reached for the chicken. I wasn't aware Johnnie was watching me until I heard him chuckle at the head of the table where he sat. "I like you, Preacher," he said. "Most preachers reach for the chicken first." Then everyone laughed. I was thankful I had passed another test.

There was little other conversation at the table. No one excused himself, but pushed back and left as soon as he finished. There were other hungry people waiting for a place at the table. We went outside to pick our teeth and visit.

††††††

MOUNTAIN PLUMBING

The postmaster motioned for me to come over to the post office corner of the general store to see something that had come in the mail. Lying among the pile of packages was a coil of shiny copper pipe from Sears Roebuck and Company. I grinned and said, "I guess Terry is planning to repair his plumbing." She laughed.

At that time, our mission parsonage had the only indoor plumbing in the area. The sheriff had shot Terry's plumbing full of holes about a month ago so now everyone along the mail route knew Terry was about to go into business again.

I spent the night with bootleggers and moonshiners without fear. They knew I minded my own business. I never asked questions, but had been put on the spot. She wanted me to know what was going on. Terry had caused problems and the peace-loving people wanted him to stay out of business. So for the first time I called the sheriff to report a still. Rex said, "I'll wait until he gets it set up, then I'll hit him again." To my knowledge, no more plumbing ever came by mail.

WHITE FLIES

Doctor Wagers had grown up in the Mill Creek Community, and though he practiced medicine in Manchester, he was very interested in raising the health standards of his home community.

Flies were a big problem in the summer time. Hog lots, barnyards, and outhouses were breeding places and the flies multiplied. I usually stayed with Dave and Pearl Hubbard, who ran the Brightshade Post Office and general store. The roomy house was next door, and though their doors and windows were screened, the flies waited by the door to get in as it opened many times during the day. Fly swatters and fly paper were used, and still they came. The ones that survived stayed on the ceilings at night. As I went to bed and looked up, I wondered how they landed upside down since they didn't fly upside down.

Many of the homes did not have screens, so Doc Wagers held a community meeting to urge all to screen their homes and sprinkle lime in their outhouses. Some of the oldtimers chuckled, "Why pay for expensive screens when the old woman can shoo the flies off the table with a branch while we eat?" But one of them decided he would at least get a bag of lime and sprinkle some in the privy every day. "Might cut down the smell when the breeze shifts towards the house," he thought.

In a few days, he surprised Doc Wagers when he walked into his office and announced: "Wal, I decided to do what you said and put screens on my winders." "What caused you to change your mind?" Doc asked. "Wal, I started putting lime in my outhouse, and after awhile I began seeing all these white flies on my dinner table."

††††††

FIVE CORN

During the time I was working at Mill Creek to finish the church-house, I would eat lunch at Hubbard's and visit with the whittlers and shoppers. It was illegal to gamble in the county but I observed a lanky, thin-cheeked man of indeterminate age who sometimes came by to play a strange game. They called him "Five Corn." As nearly as I could tell, the game was played much like rolling dice. Five kernels of corn were used with part of them marked with a pencil on the germ side. Wagers were made on how many marks turned up or down when thrown on a smooth surface.

"Five Corn" made enough to keep in "backy" and snacks and the law had tried to catch him. Most people humored him, thinking he wasn't "all there," or "plumb shaller." One day, a deputy saw him playing with a group, and started their way. Five Corn saw him and, slipping one of the kernels into his pocket, and shushing the others, kept on playing with only four kernels of corn. He and the others were brought before the judge on the charge of playing "Five Corn." "I caught him red-handed this time, Yer Honor," the deputy declared. The judge turned to Five Corn. "Guilty, or not guilty?" "Not guilty, Yer Honor." "You were observed playing Five Corn. How can you say that?" "Beg to differ, Yer Honor. I have witnesses that we were playing 'Four Corn' not 'Five Corn.' We used only four kernels." The other players nodded in agreement. The judge glowered at the hapless deputy. "Case dismissed!" People quit calling Five Corn "plumb shaller" after that.

††††††

I'LL QUIT BEFORE I VIOLATE

There was a feeling among some mountain folks that as long as he didn't get caught, he hadn't violated the law. Lillie Bowling was a good law-abiding citizen. He and his wife, Martha, were faithful church members, and often had the preacher's family over for Sunday dinner. Lillie might take a little drink now and then, but thought nothing of it. Some of the Jack's Creek young men had a still up the holler, and since Lillie had a good mule and sled, asked him if he would haul a load of meal to the still. Lillie studied about it a few minutes, then decided there could be no harm in that, and agreed. After he got the meal to the still, the boys said, "Why don't you stay and help us work up the mash." Lillie replied, "Nope, I'm going to quit before I violate." And he went back home with his mule and sled.

Word got back to the preacher, so when he was invited over for Sunday dinner again, they were finishing and Lillie urged the preacher to have another helping of food. Porterfield pushed his chair back and said, "Nope, I'm going to quit before I violate." Lillie's mouth opened in surprise. "Where did ye hear that?" he asked. Everyone laughed. I never heard of Lillie fooling with the still all the time I was at Jack's Creek.

CHAPTER XIX

A NEW CHURCH AND "FAITH"

Ed Gabbard was a generous lumberman from Winchester who had a lumbermill near Mill Creek. I was riding over from Jack's Creek for services once a month. We were meeting in the two-room school. The school burned one night and we had no meeting place. Ed Gabbard challenged me. "I hear you are a builder. If you can raise enough money to dry kiln and plane the lumber, I'll furnish every piece of rough lumber you need to build a church." Ed even helped me raise the money by riding with me to see local people and Manchester businesses he traded with. We soon had over $600 raised; enough for everything including doors and windows, wiring, roof, and paint.

I was architect, contractor, builder, carpenter, electrician, painter, and mason. The community men worked with me. I hired one man to build the chimney. Within six months, we had a pretty white church with steeple and bell nestled against the foot of the hill. I laid oak floors, beaded walls and ceilings. We even got church members together and built our own pews, communion table and pulpit. The members said, "This is our church. We built it."

But the ones who really sacrificed, were Dave and Pearl Hubbard, who donated the land and boarded the preacher and his horse for six months. And Jessie, who milked the cow, fed pigs and chickens, and was practically a widow for the six months.

It was a gala occasion when the church was dedicated. People

Dedication of Mill Creek Church—1940

came from everywhere. Bishop Praetorius, Superintendent
Lehman and other staff members came from Beverly. It was
a time of rejoicing and feasting. Ed Gabbard met Jessie and told
her he wanted her to come over with me. "I've got a young
mare my daughter in Winchester is afraid to ride. If you'll ride
her, I'll give her to you."

It was an offer we couldn't turn down. Jessie asked me,
"How can we feed another horse?" "By faith," I replied. So
the four-year-old chestnut mare arrived by truck, and we named
her Faith. She had a beautiful star in her forehead. She stood
only fourteen hands next to Dixie's fifteen hands, but she had
the smoothest gait I had ever ridden. Compared to Dixie, it
was like riding in a limosine instead of a truck.

Jessie was right at home riding her, and Ed Gabbard was

pleased. One of our hardest tasks when we left Jack's Creek was to part with Dixie and Faith.

"Dixie" and "Faith" at Jack's Creek.
Our two transportation mares for Jessie and me.

††††††

CALLED TO GO TO MORE DISTANT FIELDS

The superintendent of our mission in Nigeria, Africa, stopped to visit us. "Are you still willing to go to Africa?" he asked. "We need you badly." "We'll go where God leads," was our reply. So the appointment came, and in September, 1940, we left our beloved people for a year's training in Missionary Medicine in New York City, prior to sailing for Nigeria. (Note: Due to the threat of World War II we never left the United States.)

PHOTO ALBUM

Roscoe and Jessie riding double
on Dixie.

A well broken oxen made a reliable steed.

Pa Lewis forging a mule shoe

A young boy happy with
his picture book from the
Mission book mobile

The first log house built on Red Bird River near
Jacks Creek

Collett boys quartet from Upper Jacks Creek

Youth night at Jacks Creek

The Plowmans at Jacks Creek in 1955
Kent, Roscoe, Phyllis, Kay and Jessie

Grinding cane

Jessie carried the
mail on Faith—1940

Red Bird Mission Staff—1939
Lower Right—Supt. Lehman; Lower Left—Roscoe Plowman;
Lower Center—Dr. Raymond and Naomi Nelson;
Far Upper Left—Jessie Plowman

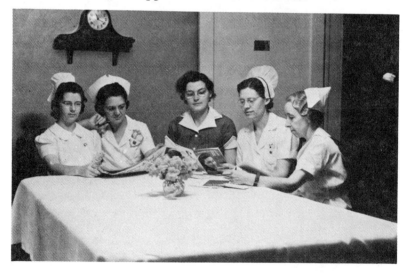

Nursing staff of the Red Bird Mission Hospital—1939

Charlie Collett and Ed Moffatt cutting a virgin poplar

A working—clearing a hillside to plant corn between logs

A one room school group put on a Christmas program
They later received toys and candy

Taylor Sizemore preaching at a Jacks Creek Memorial

Nan Collett carding wool at the Jacks Creek Center

A sled made without nails or glue

Sudie Gee drawing water from her well

An old grave yard

PART II

SECOND TIME AROUND

CHAPTER I

WE RETURN TO JACK'S CREEK

A great deal had transpired since we left the creek in 1940. John and Donna Bischoff were appointed from Illinois to take our place. We had been turned back from Africa by the threat of war. We filled in at one of our Italian mission stations in Wisconsin until I was accepted as a chaplain in the Army Air Corps. After four years of service in Texas and the European Theater, I returned to Wisconsin as a major in the Reserves and superintendent of the Italian Mission. My family had grown. Kent had been born in 1941, in Wisconsin, and Kay in 1943 in Texas.

I couldn't get Kentucky out of my blood, so when Bischoffs were appointed superintendent of the mission and Jack's Creek was open in 1948, I asked to return. This time the roads were better, and we were moved in by truck. It had grown. Some had left for school and work. Others had married and settled here. We had new teachers, a new doctor, and several other new staff members. Leonard had died, but Ruth, now a widow, was still postmaster and keeping store. Taylor was still bringing in the mail by mule. The Bringardner Mill had left and the tracks removed, leaving a partial road bed. My transportation now was a used army jeep. The river still had to be forded up to where the mill had been and down five miles to Flat Creek. The long trips to Mill Creek and Queendale were no longer on my circuit. Arthur and Esther Russell were now stationed at Mill Creek and served Spring Creek as well. My greatest loss was Dixie.

It was told that she was still living—she would be fifteen—I was afraid that finding her would be too emotional. The Frontier Nurses had "Faith," the little mare that had been given Jessie before we left Jack's Creek in 1940.

The jeep was handy, but more expensive to keep up and "feed." The universal joints kept wearing out on the drive shaft until I learned that fording the river so much got sand in them. I began to carry a grease gun and instead of having to rub my mount down as before, I crawled under the jeep and greased all the joints to squeeze out all the water and sand. This saved a lot of repairs.

But I still missed having a horse. When I learned that one of our members in Indiana had a five-gaited brood mare with papers and a stallion foal I could get for about $150, I took young Manford and the mission truck and went after them. They filled the void I had for Dixie.

This section will be abbreviated to include only unusual experiences and those that were impressed upon my memory. There will be many happenings left out and dear friends not mentioned. They are all nonetheless important to Jessie and me.

Leaving Phillip's Fork meeting in Plowman jeep
on bedrock road—1948.

CHAPTER II

A GREAT MAN IN A SMALL BODY

We found we had more time to spend with Upper Jacks Creek and Bowens Creek people since my more distant circuits had been eliminated.

Most of the Upper Jacks Creek folks were Colletts. Charlie and Laura Collett were well-known for their grocery store and logging operations. Laura taught school for many years. Their large family of children did well in school and in trades and professions. We were always welcome there as well as in the other fine homes of Charlie's brothers.

Jessie and the Jacks Creek teachers helped in their Sunday School each week. I preached on special Sundays.

Allen Collett, one of Charlie's brothers, had been crippled in his younger years, perhaps by polio, and now his body was withered and hunched and he was confined to getting around the house in a hickory bottom chair. Allen would tilt back with his hands grasping the rungs on either side and walk the chair anywhere there was a solid floor. He wore off the back legs of several chairs in his lifetime.

Allen had a brilliant mind and was determined to develop it. Getting all the law books he could, he studied until his legal skill was recognized throughout the whole area. He helped a lot of people who needed legal advice.

Allen became a dedicated Christian before we returned to Jacks Creek. He studied the Scriptures as zealously as he had studied law. He was a leading preacher and an excellent Bible teacher. His heart was so full of love that we were always greeted with a hug as we bent over within his reach. He became pastor of the Upper Jacks Creek church and we worked together in harmony.

We were invited to attend a meeting in one of the homes one night. Allen was in charge. There was a beautiful spirit. I was asked to preach. As I stood up I saw preacher Shelby. I turned to him and said, "Shelby, there was a time when we were not in harmony. But when we left, you and I were brothers." Shelby jumped to his feet and stepping up beside me, put his arm around me and said to the congregation, "We still are brothers."

As Allen became older and roads got better, he felt that his congregation should become a part of the Lower Jacks Creek membership. This added greatly to the witness of the church on the whole creek. Charlie and Laura fitted right in with their leadership.

But Allen Collett did so much for both communities in those years, in spite of his handicap, that I must place him among the many great men of the mountains.

Preacher Allen Collett
in the Upper Jack's Creek schoolhouse doorway.

CHAPTER III

THE TRUANT TEACHER

Our Phyllis was fifteen when we returned to Jack's Creek. Kent was seven and Kay was five. Phyllis attended the Mission High School by boarding at the Center. I transported her and other Jack's Creek students home for the weekends. After graduation, Phyllis tried college, but came home at mid-year saying she was not cut out for college.

It was Christmas, and the young new teacher at Phillips Fork didn't like her job. She didn't show up half of the time. The children liked it, but not the parents. Before Christmas, the teacher had held a "box supper" to raise money for treats for the children. When she took the money to town to buy the treats, she never returned. The school board asked Phyllis to complete the year. She shrugged and said, "I'll try."

It was three miles to the school. I had no horse at the time, and couldn't spare the jeep. I finally found an old nag that would do, and a cheap Eastern saddle. The only times Phyllis missed school was when the water was too high to ford.

The parents said, "Phyllis teaches school. T'other teacher just kept school when she felt like it." For the first time in a long time, the children were learning something. There was just one problem. Some of the older boys didn't like going to school so steadily. They tried turning her horse loose and running him off. Phyllis was after dark getting home once. She tried taking a shortcut and got lost. Though she had to walk several times, and I had to find her horse, she never quit. Once I found the horse with a bullet in its back. The wound healed. Phyllis kept on teaching. Once, the boys put a skunk under the schoolhouse, thinking she would send them home. She made them crawl under the building and drag it out. She taught the rest of the day, and the children had to endure the smell along with their teacher.

The parents backed her all the way, and asked her to come back next year. But Phyllis had other plans. She wanted to be a nurse or an x-ray technician. She enrolled in Cincinnati and became a registered x-ray technician.

Phillip's Fork School
Phyllis Plowman and her students.

CHAPTER IV

THE CRIPPLING JEEP RIDE

Thomas and his woman lived on the edge of two counties and it was told that he received welfare checks from both. Since he was "drawing" for disability, it was necessary to have a statement from a doctor in that county to renew his application from time to time. Thomas' cabin was in Leslie County but he needed to comply with a request to get a statement from the Clay County doctor at Manchester. He learned I was driving my jeep in to Manchester, and asked if he could ride along. There was room so I agreed.

Thomas looked fine to me. And when I stopped at the house. he came out with a big smile, hopped in the front seat next to me and said, "I shore do thank ye for takin' the trouble to tote me to the doctor." We drove the twenty-five miles in and out of the river and over Flat Creek Mountain to State Highway 80. We called it "suicide drive." It was so-named by a Courier Journal correspondent who had had a harrowing experience driving between Manchester and Hyden. The non-union truckers were paid by the number of loads of coal they hauled to the tipple, not by the hour. Each driver tried to beat the other as they passed each other on hills and around curves on the two lane road. I learned to hit the ditch when I saw two trucks coming side by side and no place to go.

Well, when I got Thomas to the doctor's office, a terrible thing had happened to him. He could hardly move. I helped him out of the jeep and into the office where he collapsed on a chair. I'm sure his welfare application was renewed. He perked up as soon as he got home.

CHAPTER V

AUNT DELIE'S GALL BLADDER

Aunt Delie, a small woman, kept having sick spells. She had a lot of pain, and could not keep anything on her stomach when these attacks occurred. Doc suspected gall stones, but she refused to go to the hospital for x-rays. One day Aunt Delie had the worst spell of all. Doc was away, so Wiley came for me. When I got there, the neighbors were sitting around the room waiting for her to die.

I tried giving a sedative by mouth, but she couldn't keep it down. I learned at the Medical School that morphine was soluble in water, so hurrying home (Jessie was away) I boiled some water. Taking a teaspoon, I sterilized it, then dissolved a morphine tablet in the spoon with the sterile water. Drawing this solution up in a syringe, and armed with cotton and alcohol, I headed back to Aunt Delie. With Wiley's permission, I injected the morphine in her frail arm. Soon she was sleeping like a baby. The neighbors went home. Wiley and I watched by the bedside. I had done some considerable praying and told the Lord, "That is all I know to do." When Aunt Delie awoke after a long sleep, she was fine and wanted to get up. The Lord had heard my desperate prayer, for Aunt Delie never had another attack. She was as spry as she could be and called me her "Little Doctor."

CHAPTER VI

BILLY'S DREAM

It was the "edge of dark" when a knock was heard on our clinic door and a voice out of the past called my name. Billy was standing on the side porch. I invited him in out of the chilly air. We greeted each other warmly. It had been over nine years since Jessie and I had seen Billy. He looked thinner and older.

Billy had just arrived that day and wanted to share a dream that he had had. The Scriptures speak of a number of dreams and their interpretations, and our folks put a great deal of stock in dreams and their meaning. "A terrible tide was raging down Jack's Creek," Billy began. "I fell in way up the creek. I struggled to swim out, but couldn't. Pap tried to save me and failed. As I was swept along, others tried to rescue me and failed. As I neared here, I saw you and called, and you swam in and saved me," Billy continued. "When I woke up, I knew I had been dreaming. Then the interpretation came to me. Pap and Mammy with all their love, couldn't save me. Kinfolk, neighbors, and preachers couldn't save me. Then you came along, Mr. Plowman. One of these days you are going to baptize me."

Perhaps I should have urged him to follow through immediately. I waited, and he became involved in some of the old life again. In later years, I remembered the dream. I drove to Jack's Creek again. Slicky John was dead, but Betty still kept the store. A hard-working mountain woman ages quickly but after thirty years, changed very slowly. Betty looked the same as she did when we lived there. We embraced in tearful greeting. "Where's Billy?" I asked. "He was up at Pap's old place awhile ago." Pap and Mammy were dead. I drove a piece, then walked. Billy was there, his back to me; a mule's hoof between his knees, a hammer in his hand, doing what he could do so well. I waited until he finished with the shoe, then spoke. "Billy!" He whirled. "Wal, I'll be, ifin hit ain't Mr. Plowman," he blurted. "You're lookin' good, Billy." We talked about old times for awhile, then I asked, "Billy, when are you going to let me baptize you?" He studied a minute, then replied, "One of these days—one of these days."

NOTE: Ruth, Billy's sister told me at my last visit that Billy had finally been converted and was baptized. He asked for me but thought I was too far away to come. Little did he know that I would have traveled across many miles to have fulfilled his dream.

CHAPTER VII

THE COLONEL AND THE WEATHERBY TRAIL

I must go back to earlier days to pick up the beginning of this story. Preacher Willis Sizemore, "Uncle Willis" was a loyal friend of Superintendent Lehman and the Red Bird Mission. He loved the Lord and no one could talk to him more than one minute without him speaking of the Lord. Uncle Willis was a "Hardshell" Baptist. Once in Grace, always in Grace. "A wedding performed in Heaven and no divorce" he would say. The Bible schollar, Spurgeon, was a favorite writer and he named one of his sons after him. Trouble in the family caused the two brothers to slip away and live in California. They never returned. Uncle Willis had his casket made and his grave stone carved with everything but date of death, and stored it away.

The boys in California sent for him to come for a visit. He died while there, and was buried there. I stored the stone in our barn and used the casket for a poor widow's burial who was about his size. The stone was later used in the walls of the new church.

T. C. came out of all the trouble as an orphaned son and grandson of Uncle Willis. He was practically brought up by the mission and eventually graduated from our high school. Whenever he got in trouble, Superintendent Lehman would say, "Remember how far he has come."

We lost track of him while we were away, but I believe he graduated from Union College. When we returned, T. C. was teaching school at Bear Creek. This was a one room school in a small settlement at the end of nowhere, overlooking the Red Bird Valley.

T. C. had ability. He was a promoter by nature and determined that he was going to be somebody and to put Bear Creek School on the map. A one room school at the end of a ridge in the wilderness? Well, he did it!

The Bear Creek precinct was solid Republican as were all of the surrounding precincts. The only way to the nearest town, Manchester, was over a rough wagon trail. They needed a road, but the governor was a Democrat. Undaunted, T. C. made a trip to Frankfort and got an audience with the governor. As the governor looked at this young country fellow from the hollers of Eastern Kentucky, he inquired, "What can I do for you, Mr. Sizemore?" "I came to give you a proposition, Governor Weatherby," T. C. countered. "We badly need a road to get to our community and my school from Manchester. We are all Republicans. If I get every single Republican to register Democrat before the next election, will you build the road? We'll name it after you, sir."

The governor had never heard of anything like this before. Thinking there was no way T. C. could get all those voters to change their registration, he agreed and they shook hands. T. C. went back and convinced every Republican that the road would be worth more to them than being Republicans and they changed. T. C. carried the registration to the governor, and he honored his word. Men were soon in the area surveying, buying the right-of-way, and started the grading. When the road was graveled and ready to use, T. C. arranged a great dedication service to be held at the Bear Creek School. Dignitaries from all over the state and Governor Weatherby came. The people had a big dinner. The governor dedicated the road as the Weatherby Trail. He then personally presented T. C. with a commission as a Kentucky Colonel.

T. C. had done what he said he would. The Bear Creek School had been put on the map and he was somebody. We were no longer to call him T. C. He was now Colonel Sizemore. The Colonel launched into local politics and did well. From there he took over the Manchester newspaper. As far as I know, he is still in the newspaper work somewhere in the state. I still remember what Superintendent Lehman said of him as a boy. "Remember how far he has come."

CHAPTER VIII

A SERMON IN STONES

It fell my task to build churches during both of our tours of service at Jack's Creek Center. The Mill Creek Church was finished and dedicated before we left in 1940. The Mill Creek Center became a full-time appointment before we returned with Arthur and Esther Russell being appointed there. Spring Creek was added to it. An outside preacher was coming in to the Peabody Center way down river. So my long trips were eliminated. With only Phillips Fork, upper Jack's Creek, and Bowen's Creek left, I turned to building two more church houses.

Dedication of Bowen's Creek Church
Circa—1953

Uncle Johnnie Napier had donated land for a church on Bowen's Creek and soon a beautiful little building was dedicated. The Jack's Creek school had burned during the Bischoff's time there and they had rebuilt it with native stone. The Jack's Creek people had always used our school as a place to worship. "Why can't we have a church of our own like the rest?" they asked. "Well, why not?" And I began working on the idea.

Roads were coming closer. The Kentucky-West Virginia Power Company was building a power line to us. Our schools had been preparing our young people for high-quality service anywhere they wanted to go. Some had stayed as teachers and local support was growing. Herman, the young man who had driven the old truck when we got the load of precious hay was a World War II veteran, had graduated from Union College with high honors and was working on his master's degree while his wife taught at Jack's Creek. Herman's father-in-law was a stone mason. Herman's two younger brothers, M. D. and Taylor, were carpenters. It was all fitting into place.

As a major in the Reserves, I worked with the Veteran's Administration in Louisville to charter a school for veterans at

Veteran's school organized by Reverend Plowman for veterans of W.W. II to prepare them for G.E.D.—1949.

Jack's Creek with Herman as a teacher. About thirty veterans signed up under the GI Bill to study. I was the director and did the paper work without renumeration. Many of the men were school dropouts, ranging from second grade to tenth grade. After three years, several had passed the G.E.D. and went on to college and teaching. Not only was the school a boon to the community veterans, but also achieved a second goal. It kept Herman's family at Jack's Creek long enough to bring the father-in-law in as the church mason.

My intent was to tie every family into the physical building itself. Each family was to bring at least one stone that had meaning to them to be built into the walls where they could be seen. I was told the first grist mill to grind corn on the creek powered with a waterwheel had washed away, but the grindstone burs should be in the creek bed if they weren't buried too deeply in the gravel to find. We looked where the mill had stood and sure enough they were only partially buried, and we were able to dig them out and use them.

Ruth's old home had burned. Leonard was dead and she wanted to build a new home so the teachers could board with her. Where the grate had been in the old house was a huge hearth stone. We dug it up to go into the church wall. A nest of copperheads was found under it. The stone stoop to Lilly Bowling's house, old grind stones, stone steps, parts of stone walks, foundation stones, stepping stones, Uncle Willis' tombstone were all placed in prominent places and can be seen today if you visit the Jack's Creek Church. The giant millstones were placed on either side of the entrance to remind people that they gave them flour for their first bread on Jack's Creek but also to remind them that "Whosoever shall offend one of these little ones that believe in me, it is better for him that a millstone were hanged about his neck, and he were cast into the sea." (Mark 9:42)

Our people were then asked to hitch up their sleds and haul in all the flat stones they could find. Stones they turned over with their plows on the hills; stones they stumbled over; stones they crossed the creek on; stones in the creek the hogs plopped over every night as they rooted for crawdads.

The pile grew and the master stone mason fitted them together into the building to form a beautiful church for the worship of God.

Jack's Creek Church built in 1950
showing mill stones.

I stressed to our congregation that whether we had been stumbling blocks or stepping stones we are to be as Paul said, "Fellow citizens with the saints and of the household of God; and are built upon the foundation of the apostles and prophets, Jesus Christ Himself being the Chief Corner Stone; in whom all the building fitly formed together groweth unto an holy temple in the Lord in whom ye also are builded together for an habitation of God through the Spirit." (Eph. 2:19-11). Then I added from I Peter 2:5, "Ye also as lively stones are built up a spiritual house; an holy priesthood, to offer up spiritual sacrifices, acceptable to God by Jesus Christ."

And so the church was built and dedicated "A SERMON IN STONES."

CHAPTER IX

CONCLUSION

Should someone ask; "Have you told the whole story?" I would have to answer, "No." There are some events that should not be told even if they would probably make very interesting reading. Sometimes it is best not to open old wounds after years of healing.

There were times over the long period of our living on the Red Bird River that violence erupted and lives were taken. Some of those involved were very good friends. We helped bury the dead and comfort the bereaved. Alcohol was most always at the bottom of the trouble.

Two of my friends shot each other while at a party where the home brew had been spiked with several bottles of rubbing alcohol. Both burials were at the same time in different cemetaries. I officiated at one burial then went to the other home to try to comfort the family there.

One of our fine talented young men drank what they called "Bad" moonshine and was poisoned. "Doc" did all he could to save him but without success. Farmer prayed for forgiveness, then he called his brothers and sisters together along with other friends and preached to them. He begged them to not drink any more moonshine and to live Christian lives. His face showed the peace in his heart when he died. Farmer had one of the most beautiful voices I have heard as he played his guitar and sang the old mountain ballads. His fame had gone beyond the hills and there were those who came and recorded some of his music for posterity. He probably could have gone on to greater recognition, but for the rude ending of his life.

Once I was called to the home of a friend in the middle of the night. He had shot a man in self defence while they were drinking. The dead man was lying on his face on the floor. A pool of blood was spreading out from his chest. We carried him outside on the porch and I called the sheriff. The circuit judge advised that my friend take his family and leave the area for a while, which he did.

Only once can I remember praying that someone would not attend church. I was at my Spring Creek appointment on a Saturday afternoon. A son of my host came from Manchester much distraught. He said that for once he had gone to town without his gun. While there he met a man with an old grudge who told him he better go home, get his gun and come back if he didn't want to get shot down in cold blood. His parting words were; "If you don't come back I'll come out to church Sunday and we'll settle our differences then." That was when I started praying, "Lord, please keep this man from church tomorrow." The son took his gun to church Sunday but my prayers were answered. The man from Manchester never showed up.

Some have asked us, "Weren't you afraid to live in the Kentucky hills?" I always told them that I knew of no safer place to live. We knew of no one who wanted to harm us. We never locked our doors at night. We were never robbed. Our tools and equipment in the barn and sheds were never touched. Some prankish boys got into our chicken house one Saturday night and slipped off with four or five old laying hens to have a chicken roast up the holler. I had a good idea who they were but never said a word. I figured they had suffered enough trying to eat those old tough hens that I had recently dipped in lice disenfectant. Sheep dip just won't wash off.

We now live near the city of Louisville. Jessie and I are much aware that our lives are in danger every time we drive to town.

Fifty thousand people are killed every year on our highways because of drinking drivers. We have been hit twice by drunks. Fortunately, only our cars were damaged and we escaped. Homes have been robbed in the area. We always bolt our doors before retiring at night. I keep a shotgun beside my bed. "Afraid?" I have lived in only two places where I never thought of being in danger—Among our friends at Jack's Creek and in my boyhood home in the hills of Oregon.

We have lived twelve wonderful years at Jack's Creek on Red Bird River. Jessie and I have been enriched as well as our children; Phyllis, Kent, and Kay, by these years and by our people there. I know of no finer people on the face of the earth.

I hope no one feels hurt or offended by any of the accounts or because they were not mentioned. I have purposely changed names or used only first names in some instances. I kept no journal of events during those years, and after three or four decades may have made some mistakes. I have been as factual as I can remember. I hope that all who read this will have a higher reverence for our Appalachian people, their customs, and their culture.

Jack's Creek Center—1952

Greedy people are ripping up our beautiful hills and polluting the once-clear fish inhabited streams with their strip mines. I want to remember these beautiful mountains and the people as we found them in the thirties and fourties when we were "Twice Out of Sight."

GLOSSARY

BABY—Youngest child regardless of age.

BACKY—Chewing tobacco; usually home made twist.

BREAD—Corn bread

CLEVER—Hospitable

COMMON—Feeling well

DIDDLERS—Baby chicks

DRAWING—Receiving monthly check from the governemnt.

EDGE OF DARK—Dusk

FODDER—Dried corn leaves

GRANNY—Mid-wife

GRATE—Coal burning fireplace

LAID BY—Last corn hoeing

LAW—Sheriff

LEAST ONE—Youngest infant

MEAL—Corn flour

MEMORIAL—Graveside service in honor of a family patriarch

MESS—Especially tasty (Mess of pottage)

NUBBINS—Short ears of corn

PIED—Spotted

PLUMBING—Copper coil of moonshine still.

PLUM SHALLER— Mentally deficient

POKE—Sack or bag

PRETTY—Plaything or toy.

RIGHT SMART— Considerable

SALAT—Wild fresh
greens

SEVERAL—Plenty

SHOAT—Young hog

SHUCK BEANS—Beans
dried in their hulls

SLIPPERS—Low cut
shoes

STONE DEAD—Injured
badly or knocked un-
conscious

TIDE—Flood

UNDER THE POWER—
Gripped by the Spirit
shown by fast
sustained preaching

WAKE—All night vigil
for the dead

WHITE EYE—Exhausted

WOMAN—Wife

YOUNGUNS—Small
children